Spring Harvest Bible Workbook

ACTS
Building a People of Faith

Ian Coffey and Ruth Dearnley

Series editor for thematic workbooks – Jeff Lucas

Authentic

SPRING HARVEST

Equipping the Church for action

11 10 09 08 07 06 05   7 6 5 4 3 2 1

First published in 2005 by Spring Harvest Publishing Division and Authentic Media
9 Holdom Avenue, Bletchley, Milton Keynes, Bucks, MK1 1QR, UK
and 129 Mobilization Drive, Waynesboro, GA 30830-4575, USA

www.authenticmedia.co.uk

British Library Cataloguing in Publication Data

A catalogue record for this book is available from the British Library

ISBN 1-85078-616-X

Typeset by Spring Harvest
Cover design by Diane Bainbridge
Print management by Adare Carwin
Printed and Bound by J. H. Haynes & Co. Ltd., Sparkford

CONTENTS

ABOUT THIS BOOK

This workbook is written primarily for use in a group situation, but can easily be used by individuals who want to study the book of Acts.

▶ The emphasis of the studies will be on the application of the Bible. Group members will not just learn facts, but will be encouraged to think: 'How does this apply to me or in my church setting? Does it require a change in my/our thinking?'
▶ The aim of the studies is not to find the 'right answer', but to help members understand what the passage is saying by working through the questions. The Christian faith throws up paradoxes and events in people's lives may make particular verses challenging. The questions are designed to help people talk honestly about their questions and experiences.
▶ There is a difference between being a collection of individuals who happen to meet together every Wednesday and being an effective group who bounce ideas off each other, sparking inspiration and creativity. The process of working through these studies will encourage healthy group dynamics.

This book will not tell you what to think, but it will help you discover the truth of God's word through thinking, discussing, praying and listening.

The New International Version of the text is printed in the workbook.

FOR GROUP MEMBERS

▶ You will get more out of the study if you spend some time during the week reading the Bible passage and the commentary on the text. Make a note of anything you don't understand.

▶ Pray that God will help you to understand the passage and show you how to apply it. Pray for other members in the group too.

▶ Be willing to take part in the discussions. The leader of the group is not there as an expert with all the answers. They will want everyone to get involved and share their thoughts and opinions.

▶ However, don't dominate the group! If you are aware that you are saying a lot, make space for others to contribute. Be sensitive to other group members and aim to be encouraging.

FOR INDIVIDUALS

▶ Although this book is written with a group in mind, it can also be used by individuals. Consider how you would answer the questions and write your thoughts down as you work through the studies.

▶ You may find it helpful to talk to a prayer partner about what you have learnt, and ask them to pray for you as you try and apply what you are learning to your life.

▶ The workbook can also be read straight through as a commentary on key texts in Acts by omitting the questions.

INTRODUCTION

People who achieve are always worth studying.

The first followers of Jesus earned a reputation for shaking their world and within a generation their message spread across the Roman Empire. This was an extraordinary achievement. There were no mass communications or media campaigns and few of the first followers of Christ could claim to be influential. It certainly wasn't fashionable to line up behind a peasant Jewish carpenter who ended up nailed to a cross as a troublemaker.

Yet their message and influence spread like a forest fire.

Why?

Thirty Remarkable Years

Three crucial decades in world history. That is all it took. In the years between AD *33 and 64 a new movement was born. In those 30 years it got sufficient growth and credibility to become the largest religion the world has ever seen and to change the lives of hundreds of millions of people. It has spread to every corner of the globe ... and has had an indelible impact on civilisation, on culture, on education, on medicine, on freedom and of course on the lives of countless people worldwide. And the seedbed for all this, the time when it took decisive root, was in these three decades. It all began with a dozen men and a handful of women and then the Spirit came.*

Acts for Today, Michael Green (Hodder and Stoughton, 1993, p 10)

The Holy Spirit worked through the lives of these ordinary people. What kind of people were they? What sort of challenges did they fear? What qualities did they demonstrate? And what lessons can we learn from their lives?

The studies in this workbook take us through some snapshots from the book of Acts that offer some answers to these questions. The discussion pointers and questions help translate the experience of the 1st century Christians for 21st century Christians. It was a challenge to live as a disciple of Christ in Rome or Corinth or Ephesus. It remains a challenge today to live out our faith in Rotherham, Colchester or Ealing.

These studies are designed to help us think about how we face those challenges and how we can be prepared by God to meet them.

The first followers of Christ saw the message about Jesus touch and transform people in their multi-faith and often hostile culture. And by God's grace we can see the same today in our world. They were available for God to use and that is all he asks of us. His Spirit is the same now as then and his desire to touch and change lives for good remains undimmed.

Some have commented that the book of Acts doesn't finish at chapter 28 for the story continues to be recorded in each new generation of followers of Christ around the globe. Whatever chapter number we are up to now, may it record a story of vision, passion, courage, faith, commitment, promise and hope in our generation.

The Story Continues
> God is still engaged in this dynamic enterprise. He has not given up on us. That is why the study of Acts remains so important. If those first Christians could accomplish so much in so short a space of time with such skimpy resources, what might the worldwide church today accomplish if only it was prepared for the vision, the faith and the dedication they exhibited?
>
> Acts for Today (p 12)

PEOPLE OF VISION

 AIM: To catch God's vision for ourselves and his church

READ Acts 11:1-30

The apostles and the brothers throughout Judea heard that the Gentiles also had received the word of God. So when Peter went up to Jerusalem, the circumcised believers criticised him and said, You went into the house of uncircumcised men and ate with them.

Peter began and explained everything to them precisely as it had happened: "I was in the city of Joppa praying, and in a trance I saw a vision. I saw something like a large sheet being let down from heaven by its four corners, and it came down to where I was. I looked into it and saw four-footed animals of the earth, wild beasts, reptiles, and birds of the air. Then I heard a voice telling me, 'Get up, Peter. Kill and eat.'

"I replied, 'Surely not, Lord! Nothing impure or unclean has ever entered my mouth.'

"The voice spoke from heaven a second time, 'Do not call anything impure that God has made clean.' This happened three times, and then it was pulled up to heaven again.

"Right then three men who had been sent to me from Caesarea stopped at the house where I was staying. The Spirit told me to have no hesitation about going with them. These six brothers also went with me, and we entered the man's house. He told us how he had seen an angel appear in his house and say, 'Send to Joppa for Simon who is called Peter. He will bring you a message through which you and all your household will be saved.'

"As I began to speak, the Holy Spirit came on them as he had come on us at the beginning. Then I remembered what the Lord had said: 'John baptised with water, but you will be baptised with the Holy Spirit.' So if God gave them the same gift as he gave us, who believed in the Lord Jesus Christ, who was I to think that I could oppose God?"

When they heard this, they had no further objections and praised God, saying, "So then, God has granted even the Gentiles repentance unto life."

Now those who had been scattered by the persecution in connection with Stephen travelled as far as Phoenicia, Cyprus and Antioch, telling the message only to Jews. Some of them, however, men from Cyprus and Cyrene, went to Antioch and began to speak to Greeks also, telling them the good news about the Lord Jesus. The Lord's hand was with them, and a great number of people believed and turned to the Lord.

News of this reached the ears of the church at Jerusalem, and they sent Barnabas to Antioch. When he arrived and saw the evidence of the grace of God, he was glad and encouraged them all to remain true to the Lord with all their hearts. He was a good man, full of the Holy Spirit and faith, and a great number of people were brought to the Lord.

Then Barnabas went to Tarsus to look for Saul, and when he found him, he brought him to Antioch. So for a whole year Barnabas and Saul met with the church and taught great numbers of people. The disciples were called Christians first at Antioch.

During this time some prophets came down from Jerusalem to Antioch. One of them, named Agabus, stood up and through the Spirit predicted that a severe famine would spread over the entire Roman world. (This happened during the reign of Claudius.) The disciples, each according to his ability, decided to provide help for the brothers living in Judea. This they did, sending their gift to the elders by Barnabas and Saul.

TO SET THE SCENE
History has certain hinge moments when a significant incident occurs that sparks a chain reaction.

For example, Franz Ferdinand Archduke of Austria was visiting Sarajevo with his wife Sophie in June 1914 when a young Serbian nationalist shot them. Austria responded by attacking Serbia and so the First World War began and millions were caught up in the conflagration that followed.

And in recent years many of us watched in astonishment as the infamous Berlin Wall was pulled down – brick by brick – signalling the end of the Cold War and the opening up of Eastern Europe to the rest of the world.

Luke wrote the book of Acts as the second volume in his account about Jesus, and chapters 10 and 11 signal a hinge moment of history. The first followers of Jesus were Jews and they assumed that the message of good news that had touched their lives was exclusively for the people of Israel. All the non-Jews were lumped under the title Gentiles and it was assumed they had no place in God's rescue plan that centred in the death and resurrection of Jesus.

But God's vision was bigger than theirs.

Acts chapter 10 records the remarkable story of how Peter finds himself led by the Holy Spirit to the home of a Roman military officer by the name of Cornelius. It was unthinkable for a Jew to enter the home of a Gentile – they were unclean in God's eyes and contact with them would pass that uncleanness on. But Peter had a lesson to learn that God's rescue plan stretched far beyond the nation of Israel to encompass the whole world – even those who might be seen as beyond the pale.

Chapter 11 sees the lesson and its implications spreading wider still. The chapter teaches us about vision and its crucial importance for the people of God. Vision is a much used (and often abused) word. In this study we are using it to mean a sense of God-given direction.

Let's take a moment to ask ourselves whether we are a people of vision.

▶ How do you understand the word 'vision' in this context?
▶ Have there been times in your life when you had a sense that God gave you a direction to travel in?
▶ Can you identify other hinge moments in history? Have there been personal hinge moments in your own life - for example, conversion, marriage, redundancy, illness, career move.
▶ Is your church 'a people of vision'?

We begin to identify with Peter as we too sense that we are at a 'hinge moment' in the life of the church in this country. We yearn to see God's vision for us and believe that once again God's vision is bigger than ours.

Be expectant and read on.

There are four lessons about vision woven into the thread of Luke's story.

1. Vision is found in God (Acts 11:1–18)

Peter is criticised for his scandalous behaviour in entering the home of a Gentile and receiving hospitality (11:1–3). This behaviour cast serious doubts on his suitability to be regarded as a leader worthy of respect. But those who were scandalised by his actions at least had the courtesy and openness to listen to Peter's explanation.

> When significant change is suggested in church, especially if it is a change to a long-held tradition, it can be seen and talked about as 'scandalous'. What issues are affecting your church at the moment? What can we learn from Peter's behaviour and process here to help us deal with the effects of such change?

Peter offers an explanation of what had happened (11:4–15). It is interesting to note that Luke is happy to record Peter's account in his own words although he had already given a detailed account of the circumstances in the previous chapter. He doesn't want any of us his readers to miss the details or the implications.

It all began with a puzzling vision when a hungry Peter was waiting for lunch (10:10). His daydream about food took an unfortunate turn when he began to see a vision of non-kosher animals and birds. Then a voice told him, 'Get up Peter, kill and eat'. His response was what any serious-minded Jew would make, 'Surely not Lord! Nothing impure or unclean has ever entered my mouth'.

As Peter was puzzling over this vision that was repeated three times, some men arrive at the house looking for him. The Holy Spirit directed him to go with them even though they ended up at the home of a Roman military officer. The story takes another strange twist – this god-fearing Gentile reported that an angel had interrupted his prayers and told him where to find Peter and how he had a special message of joy and hope for the officer and his family.

It is extraordinary how God seems to work out his plans in different places and through different people where our life stories seem to take strange twists and turns but have an authorship and divine plan. This is such a stong indication of God's vision, the bigger picture, being worked out.

> When have you been aware of strange twists and turns later revealing God's bigger picture being worked out in your own life? What extraordinary circumstances or 'god-incidences' have later come to light?
> Are there times when our familiar ways of doing things can hinder us from seeing or hearing what God is trying to show us or say to us? Is it possible for these things to limit God's vision?
> Can you give an example of a time God interrupted your prayers to take you somewhere new?

As Peter began to explain the message about Jesus a mini-day of Pentecost broke out in the room as this Gentile family received the Holy Spirit just as Peter and the other disciples had (Acts 2:1–13).

Peter closes his explanation with an important conclusion (11:16–17). This extraordinary set of circumstances is from God. This was exactly what Jesus had promised – God had chosen to bless the Gentiles so how could Peter or anyone else stand in his way?

The hostile audience that faced Peter originally allowed their criticism to melt into praise (11:18). This thing was far, far bigger than anyone had thought – even Gentiles are included!

Being people of vision does not mean that we need to have 64 bright ideas before breakfast and run around like scalded cats. Vision that builds the kingdom always begins with God.

▶ Re-read the story of Cornelius and see how it is filled with God-incidents (as opposed to co-incidences). Peter was following a plan bigger than his own imagination.
▶ Looking back over the past few years identify ways God has used circumstances to work out his vision in your life and in your church and community.

2. Vision feeds on flexibility (Acts 11:19–22)

Luke now shifts the focus of the unfolding story to some anonymous Christians who fled Jerusalem following the hostility that lingered after Stephen had been murdered for his faith. Wherever they went they told the story of their new-found belief in Jesus the Messiah but they confined this to the Jewish community. Some travelled to the cosmopolitan city of Antioch and shared their story with some Gentiles. Just like the Roman Cornelius, these men (who were Greeks) responded to the good news about Jesus with faith and obedience. The response was contagious and soon 'a great number of people believed and turned to the Lord' (11:21).

News filtered back to the church leaders in Jerusalem who were still coming to terms with the events surrounding the conversion of a Roman officer and his family and instead of reacting they responded. When things begin to run away from our control most of us react out of insecurity and a desire to keep a handle on what is going on. But flexibility is a mark of maturity.

These insightful leaders decided to send Barnabas to Antioch to undertake a first-hand review. This was a wise move on two counts. First, he was by nature an encourager, which was how he earned his nickname (Acts 4:36). Second, he was a native of Cyprus, the same island as the men who had shared their faith at Antioch with such astonishing results (11:20). Barnabas was unlikely to take either a fire extinguisher or a big stick with him. By choosing Barnabas for this task the leaders in Jerusalem sent - in the words of William Barclay - 'the man with the biggest heart in the church'.

Vision feeds and grows on this kind of flexibility. It does not mean we have no fixed points of belief or some 'wishy-washy anything goes' mentality. But it means a willingness to embrace change, to be open to new ideas, ready to experiment, eager to learn and open to those who have a different experience from ours.

❱ What are the signs of maturity in the Christian life?
❱ What are the signs of mature Christian leadership?

3. Vision flourishes under godly people (Acts 11:23-26)

Barnabas arrived at Antioch and recognised that what was happening was genuinely a work of God - and he did what he always did best - he encouraged them to remain strong in the faith and to be wholehearted followers of Christ. Luke adds an unsolicited character reference for Barnabas describing him as 'a good man, full of the Holy Spirit and faith' (11:24). Here was a man of true integrity and spiritual maturity - and this is directly linked to the very next phrase 'and a great number of people were brought to the Lord'. The smile of God's favour rested on Barnabas and his work for the Lord flourished.

In the New Testament a person's character - the way they lived, behaved and treated others - was seen as a vital indicator of their potential as leaders. Sometimes we fall into the trap of looking at a person's gifts as most important - but gifts without character can often produce serious flaws in an individual's leadership skills.

❱ Identify one area where you have seen your character develop and mature and identify one aspect that you still need to work on.

Barnabas was a good man - but he was also gifted by God. He had the ability to see that what the new congregation at Antioch needed was someone who could teach and explain how the Jewish Scriptures pointed to Jesus of Nazareth. He recalled that his friend Saul of Tarsus was an eloquent and skilled rabbi who had undergone a dramatic conversion. Now home in his native city of Tarsus, Saul was back at his trade of tent-making and repairs.

Barnabas takes a trip to Tarsus and recruits Saul to his team which quickly grew in size and variety (Acts 13:1). This was the farsightedness of a godly man. We have all heard the phrase 'so heavenly minded they're of no earthly use'. Yet Barnabas blends a passionate spirituality with sharp practicality. This godly man recognised for his faith and love for Christ was also a skilled encourager, enabler, strategist, talent spotter and team builder.

Great numbers flocked to hear his teaching and he sowed seeds in the life of his friend and colleague, Saul, who later became better known by his Roman name, Paul. This coincided with his emergence as an apostle or senior leader in the church. Barnabas had no small part to play in this emerging ministry of Saul of Tarsus.

The church at Antioch flourished and grew into a congregation with a vision beyond themselves. Some have described them as the first truly missional congregation – much of which was the fruit of Barnabas' wise leadership. Luke notes that the nickname Christ's ones or Christians originated in the city of Antioch where the congregation that seems to have started by accident has left a lasting legacy for the world church.

> ▶ If you are the involved in the leadership of the church, what does sharp practicality look like for you at the moment and how do you nurture your own passionate spirituality?

Vision always grows best under the care of godly people.

4. Vision follows through into action (Acts 11:27–30)
Luke concludes this section with an account of how a group of Christians turned a natural disaster into an opportunity to demonstrate a very practical dimension to their faith. It reminds us that vision is not about building castles in the air but rather putting legs on our prayers and clothing our praise with action.

A prophet named Agabus predicted that a severe famine would shortly affect the whole Roman Empire. Luke – ever the careful historian - notes that this took place during the reign of Claudius (who was emperor when Britain was invaded by the Romans) and we can pinpoint this famine to a date around AD 48.

But what is more striking than Luke's reliability is the response of the mainly Gentile church at Antioch. They realised that the coming famine would hit the Christian community in and around Jerusalem where many believers were poor to begin with. In anticipation of the famine the church at Antioch began an unusual savings scheme.

Out of their own resources they put money by not for themselves, but for a group of people they had never met and who came from a different ethnic background than their own. This love gift was sent in the safe keeping of Barnabas and Saul who had the happy privilege of explaining to the senior church at Jerusalem how the junior church in Antioch had decided to express the reality that Jesus really had broken down dividing walls of traditional hostility (Eph. 2:11–18).

We can only imagine what such a gesture said to the watching world about the reality of the good news of Jesus. A faith response to a God-given vision is seen by our actions more than our words.

SUMMING UP

The call to be a people of vision is not a licence for us to pursue the latest religious bandwagon under the smokescreen 'The Lord has told me'. Acts 11 offers us a clear picture of what a God-given vision looks like.

Vision is found in God

So it follows we should pray and seek his will and plans – and listen hard for the answers.

Vision feeds on flexibility

The challenge is to openness and a willingness to lay down our own ideas and plans.

Vision flourishes under godly people

What we are is of greater importance than what we do. Developing godliness is of even greater benefit than going to the gym or jogging! (1 Tim. 4:8)

Vision follows through into action

Real visionaries are action people who are willing to get involved and dig in for the long haul. They are prepared to do and not just dream.

The story is told of an officer cadet at Sandhurst military training college who failed the course. One of his instructors had written on his report: 'The only reason anyone would follow this man is out of a sense of curiosity'.

DURING THE WEEK

Looking back over this session we began by identifying how God gives us glimpses of his vision. We have talked about how he may convey that to us and the need for church leadership and membership to be flexible and mature.

▶ What can we do this week as a faith response to the challenge to become 'a people of vision'?
>   in our own lives
>   in the life of our church
>   in our community

PRAYER AND WORSHIP

Sing the great hymn 'Be thou my vision O Lord of my heart' and use it as the basis of prayer for your community, your church and yourselves.

Spend a moment identifying and affirming the leadership team of your church. Pray for them that they too would blend a 'passionate spirituality and sharp practicality'.

PEOPLE OF PASSION

AIM

AIM: To become passionate communicators with the world we live in

READ Acts 17:16-34

While Paul was waiting for them in Athens, he was greatly distressed to see that the city was full of idols. So he reasoned in the synagogue with the Jews and the God-fearing Greeks, as well as in the market-place day by day with those who happened to be there. A group of Epicurean and Stoic philosophers began to dispute with him. Some of them asked, "What is this babbler trying to say?" Others remarked, "He seems to be advocating foreign gods." They said this because Paul was preaching the good news about Jesus and the resurrection. Then they took him and brought him to a meeting of the Areopagus, where they said to him, "May we know what this new teaching is that you are presenting? You are bringing some strange ideas to our ears, and we want to know what they mean." (All the Athenians and the foreigners who lived there spent their time doing nothing but talking about and listening to the latest ideas.)

Paul then stood up in the meeting of the Areopagus and said: "Men of Athens! I see that in every way you are very religious. For as I walked around and looked carefully at your objects of worship, I even found an altar with this inscription: TO AN UNKNOWN GOD. *Now what you worship as something unknown I am going to proclaim to you.*

"The God who made the world and everything in it is the Lord of heaven and earth and does not live in temples built by hands. And he is not served by human hands, as if he needed anything, because he himself gives all men life and breath and everything else. From one man he made every nation of men, that they should inhabit the whole earth; and he determined the times set for them and the exact places where they should live. God did this so that men would seek him and perhaps reach out for him and find him, though he is not far from each one of us. 'For in him we live and move and have our being.' As some of your own poets have said, 'We are his offspring.'

"Therefore since we are God's offspring, we should not think that the divine

being is like gold or silver or stone—an image made by man's design and skill. In the past God overlooked such ignorance, but now he commands all people everywhere to repent. For he has set a day when he will judge the world with justice by the man he has appointed. He has given proof of this to all men by raising him from the dead."

When they heard about the resurrection of the dead, some of them sneered, but others said, "We want to hear you again on this subject." At that, Paul left the Council. A few men became followers of Paul and believed. Among them was Dionysius, a member of the Areopagus, also a woman named Damaris, and a number of others.

TO SET THE SCENE

The makers of aftershaves and perfumes have concocted some exotic names to sell their products. The story is told of a woman in the pre-Christmas shopping rush asking at the perfume counter of a large department store, 'Do you have Elizabeth Taylor's *Passion*? To which the bored-looking sales assistant replied, "Madam, if I did do you think I'd still be working here?"'

Our study takes us beyond a brand name to the heart of what it means to be people who are passionate about what God wants. It involves what we see, how we feel and the manner in which we respond.

Paul – the Christian missionary and leader – visited the city of Athens, which one writer describes as the 'intellectual capital of the world'. He could have opted to play the part of a curious tourist or been mesmerised by the dazzling history of this famous city. Instead Paul chose to use the opportunity for God.

> ▶ Who do you perceive as being passionate for Jesus? Brainstorm some names of people who spring to mind and talk about why you named them?
> ▶ Do you think about your faith in terms of passion and if so how does that work, or if not why not?

Paul's passion for God was summed up by three words:
Involvement
Engagement
Discernment

Passion for God means involvement (Acts 17:16)

Involvement begins by learning to view our world as Jesus sees it.

Paul had passed through a torrid time leading up to his visit to Athens. In Philippi he had been subjected to a vicious beating and ended up in jail (16:11–23). His next port of call – Thessalonica – ended in a public riot and a hasty exit (17:5–10). His trip to Berea started well but then public agitation was again on the agenda (17:13). Paul's team concluded he needed a break in a safe haven and arranged for him to be escorted somewhere he would be less prominent in order that the dust might settle. They left him in Athens (17:15) where he could wait quietly for his travelling team to join him.

But for Paul time out didn't mean time off.

Passion was born out of pain and suffering for Paul. He had been on a perilous journey so far, but that had fired his passion for Jesus not quenched it.

▶ How do you think Paul felt as he arrived for his 'holiday'?
▶ Are you tempted to take time out from God? Or is it time out from church that you crave? What do we need to take time out from? It may be meetings, structures, busyness and other people's expectations. In what ways does your church give leaders time out?
▶ Away from the structures of church/work/home holidays can be a real opportunity to engage with God in new ways. Share with your group how you would like to see this happen.

Paul did what most visitors to Athens did – he took in the sights and sounds. But what he saw deeply disturbed him – because the city was full of idol shrines and temples (17:16).

▶ Take a brief sightseeing tour through your community. What are its strengths and weaknesses?

On the surface Athens was a city filled with splendidly designed buildings and a rich history of culture and learning. Many visitors were awed by what they saw as they toured the home of great thinkers of the past such as Socrates and Plato and the adopted city of Aristotle, Epicurus and Zeno. Here was the birthplace of democracy. Although the glory days of the Greek Empire were past even the Romans acknowledged the influence of Athens by recognising it as a free, allied city.

But Paul looked under the rug. Beyond the sophistication, learning, history and culture he spotted people living in the dark. Luke who wrote this account chooses a particular word translated by the phrase 'he was greatly distressed' (17:16). It conveys the idea of someone who is provoked or deeply disturbed. We get the English word *paroxysm* (a sudden or violent outburst). This was not mild reaction or trivial irritation – Paul was deeply affected by what he saw. Athens was a city filled with a forest of idols. A forest so dense that Paul feared they couldn't spot the wood for the trees.

> - What aspects of your community really disturb you – in Paul's words cause you to become 'greatly distressed'? What troubles you and makes you want to do something about it?
> - What sort of idols can you identify in today's culture? Consider the following statements:
>   > I'll stand as a governor at my local school because it will benefit my child.
>   > I'll have 'botox' treatment because I need to keep my good looks to be accepted and loved.
>   > I'll work these extra hours of overtime because I need to stay ahead of the pack in my career.
> - What do these statements reveal about our motives?

Paul saw the city as Jesus saw it – full of religions and ideas but empty of knowledge of the true and only God. He recognised that the many shrines and temples that filled the streets of Athens actually represented people who were lost, lonely and ruled by superstition and fear.

Involvement begins when we read the newspaper, watch the TV news, listen to the conversations that surround us every day and ask God for the special gift to view our world as Jesus sees it.

> - How does your church view your community? Does it see itself at the heart of the community or separate from it?
> - How does the community view your church?
> - List all the activities that indicate your church is involved with the community.
> - What new areas has your church become involved in over the past year?

Passion for God means engagement (Acts 17:17–21)
Engagement means discovering my marketplace and asking God to use me there.

It is interesting to see what Paul didn't do before considering his active response to what he found in Athens.

> - He didn't bury his head in the sand
> - He didn't look down his nose
> - He didn't write a prayer letter bemoaning what he saw.

All these options were open to him. He could have chosen to ignore what he saw – or felt smug and secure in his own spiritual experience. His great gifts of communication could have prompted him to write to the Christian community urging them to pray for this group of confused pagans.

Instead Paul *chose* to engage with the people around him and in a city where new ideas were two a penny (17:21) he fitted in perfectly. He got involved in the local synagogue and in the marketplace where people stopped to pass the time of day (17:17). He came across a group of philosophers who brought him to Athens' most famous debating chamber where Paul had the unique opportunity of sharing the good news about Jesus.

WHO'S WHO IN ATHENS

Athens was a city awash with ideas. Paul bumped into some influential thinkers from two quite different schools of philosophical thought.

Epicureans believed that life was all down to chance and that death was the end. The gods had no interest in what happened on earth. Living a life of pleasure was the best you could hope for. It led to a very self-centred life where pleasing no 1 was the goal.

Stoics believed that every living thing contained the spark of life that is god (pantheism) and that life was pre-programmed. Their outlook was to 'grin and bear it' no matter what life threw at you. Self-sufficiency was the highest goal.

These men were not at first impressed with Paul. The word 'babbler' (17:18) was a derogatory term for those seen as intellectually inferior. But Paul aroused enough curiosity to prompt them to invite him to address the most prestigious group in the city.

The Areopagus was a court and the city's most illustrious institution. Tradition recorded that it had been founded over 1,000 years before by the city's patron goddess, Athene. When Athens became a democracy in the 5th century BC the power of this court was broken but it retained enormous influence on matters of belief and morality. The group met on the Hill of Ares – the Greek god of war. (The Roman name for this god was Mars – so the Areopagus is sometimes called Mars Hill.)

By the time Paul made his surprise appearance the prestigious court was still held in high esteem and debated moral, educational and religious questions.

This opportunity was truly surprising – God opened a door for the gospel.

We may not possess communication gifts like Paul and we may not have the chance to speak to powerful people of influence and decision makers. But we are not relegated to become pew-sitting spectators. All of us have a marketplace where we meet people every day – the challenge is to see it as somewhere God wants to use us.

'We cannot get to the debating chamber unless we first engage in debate.'

> ❯ Now that you have talked about what idols are being worshipped around you and what disturbs you, are there things that you have:
> buried your heads in the sand
> looked down your noses at
> or moaned about from a distance?
> ❯ What is the 'our marketplace' – the place where we are challenged to make a difference? This could be office politics, gossip at the school gate, taking a stand on business ethics or risking some honest talking in your family.
> ❯ What is your church's 'marketplace'? What is working well and what could your church do better?

Passion for God means discernment (Acts 17:22–31)

Discernment is about being wise in our words and our ways.

Paul's approach in this situation teaches us about how we need wisdom, skill and sensitivity as we approach people on matters of faith – especially if they have no background of Christian faith.

First, notice how Paul begins with a positive affirmation of the Athenians' religious outlook on life. He then latches on to something he had noticed on his city tour. The Athenians had constructed an altar to an unknown god – in case they had missed one out who may be offended! Paul uses this as his starting point and sets out to fill in a gap in their knowledge. The people of Athens had acknowledged there could be a god they did not know about – so Paul sets out to make the unknown known.

Paul could have launched into an attack on the multi-faith nature of Athenian society and rebuked them for idolatry and superstition. Instead he opts for the wise approach of winning the attention of his audience. With the theme of his speech established Paul tells them some things about this unknown God.

- Go back to the sightseeing tour you went on at the beginning of this study. Did you identify any possible 'unknown god idols' on the tour?
- Remember Paul used 'the unknown god' as a starting point – a point of affirmation and connection not condemnation and alienation from the Athenians. Can you think of ways you could do the same?
- What is a possible equivalent to the idol of the unknown God in your community/work/home?

Let's look at how Paul used the unknown God idol to his advantage to reveal the true God.

God is the *creator* (17:24) of everything – so he can't be confined to a small shrine. He is the *sustainer* of all living things and does not need things such as the offerings of food brought to idol temples (17:25). He is the *ruler* of everything and governs the course of history (17:26) and far from being remote, he is the *father* who longs for his children to reach out and find him (17:27–28). He will one day *judge* the world with justice through Jesus, whose mighty resurrection is living proof that these words are true (17:31).

Nowhere does Paul quote the Old Testament scriptures (his audience would have little knowledge of them) yet everything he says is loaded with the truth of those scriptures. But he does quote two well-known Greek thinkers (17:28) to support his case.

We can learn much from Paul's approach:

- courtesy towards those listening
- clear and reasoned explanation in language that could be understood
- building a bridge into the world of his audience.

Luke's account only gives the notes of Paul's address, but there is enough here to remind us that discernment is a Spirit-given skill we all need to develop. The right word at the right time – and sometimes no words but the right actions at the right time are just what are needed.

- Identify some ways your church could develop the projects you are involved in within your community. For example, in our church we have just opened a high street shop and office centre and we are working out ways of communicating clearly who we are and why we are on the high street as well as just getting on with it.

But sharing the good news about Jesus always produces mixed response. Some of Paul's illustrious audience *laughed it off* (17:32); the very idea of life beyond death was ridiculous in their opinion. Some *put it off* (17:32) and we are not told if this was simply a lame excuse or a genuine desire to look into things further. But there was fruit (17:34) as some of Athens' high fliers found faith. Luke seems to suggest that there were not huge numbers – but then a recurring symptom of affluence and self-sufficiency is hardness of heart.

> ▶ What experiences have you had of mixed responses when you have talked about your faith or done things as a church?
> ▶ Can you identify 'fruit' from the bridges that are already being built – not necessarily quantified in large numbers but in other ways.

SUMMING UP

Paul's visit to Athens reminds us of the call to make disciples of Christ in every generation. Being people of passion means more than having a passing interest in the world around us. One church summarises this neatly with an inscription over the main exit doors of the church building: 'You are now entering the mission field'.

Involvement

We need to begin to see our world through different eyes – the eyes of Christ.

Engagement

We each have a marketplace – let's make it somewhere Jesus is welcome to work.

Discernment

Let's seek to develop the skill of being wise in our ways and our words.

The danger of studying a Bible passage such as this is that we feel it is so far removed from our everyday world. How many of us could expect to end up addressing an audience like the Areopagus? So let's earth it with a true story about influence.

In the dark days of apartheid in South Africa, a black woman was walking along the street with her small son. The boy was astonished when a white man stood aside to let them pass and even more amazed when the man lifted his hat and bid them a polite 'Good morning'. The boy noticed the man was dressed strangely and asked his mother who he was. 'That man is a priest' she told him. 'When I grow up I want to be a priest,' the boy said.

The man was Trevor Huddleston – and the boy was Desmond Tutu.

DURING THE WEEK

Think about the possible starting points of engagement you have identified in your home/work/community situation. What would be the right words or right actions to take these forward into the coming week? Talk about this in very practical terms. For example, if someone is talking about their office setting, identify a very practical action or word that would build a bridge or show a clear response.

PRAYER

Ask the members of the group to summarise opportunities they have identified in their home/work lives to build bridges. Pray for one another that as individuals and as a church we will become people of passion and influence.

PEOPLE OF COURAGE

AIM: To find God's strength to face our fears and overcome them

READ Acts 18:1-17

After this, Paul left Athens and went to Corinth. There he met a Jew named Aquila, a native of Pontus, who had recently come from Italy with his wife Priscilla, because Claudius had ordered all the Jews to leave Rome. Paul went to see them, and because he was a tentmaker as they were, he stayed and worked with them. Every Sabbath he reasoned in the synagogue, trying to persuade Jews and Greeks.

When Silas and Timothy came from Macedonia, Paul devoted himself exclusively to preaching, testifying to the Jews that Jesus was the Christ. But when the Jews opposed Paul and became abusive, he shook out his clothes in protest and said to them, "Your blood be on your own heads! I am clear of my responsibility. From now on I will go to the Gentiles."

Then Paul left the synagogue and went next door to the house of Titius Justus, a worshipper of God. Crispus, the synagogue ruler, and his entire household believed in the Lord; and many of the Corinthians who heard him believed and were baptised.

One night the Lord spoke to Paul in a vision: "Do not be afraid; keep on speaking, do not be silent. For I am with you, and no-one is going to attack and harm you, because I have many people in this city." So Paul stayed for a year and a half, teaching them the word of God.

While Gallio was proconsul of Achaia, the Jews made a united attack on Paul and brought him into court. "This man," they charged, "is persuading the people to worship God in ways contrary to the law."

Just as Paul was about to speak, Gallio said to the Jews, "If you Jews were making a complaint about some misdemeanour or serious crime, it would be reasonable for me to listen to you. But since it involves questions about words and names and your own law—settle the matter yourselves. I will not be a judge of such things." So he had them ejected from the court. Then they all turned on Sosthenes the synagogue ruler and beat him in front of the court. But Gallio showed no concern whatever.

TO SET THE SCENE

Corinth was a tough place to be a Christian.

Paul made the journey from Athens to the famous seaport of Corinth, which was only a 50-mile journey by road but a great deal further in terms of contrast between the two cities. Athens had a proud and illustrious history of culture and learning – Corinth on the other hand was rich, loud and famous for its nightlife. The Greeks coined the word 'to corinthianise' to describe corrupting someone to adopt a lifestyle dominated by drink and sex. The Greeks enjoyed theatre and in many plays a person from Corinth was typecast as a drunk. So the image of the city was not attractive.

Corinth was wealthy and its location brought traders from all over the known world. It shared Athens' multi-faith approach to religion – and its most famous goddess was Aphrodite whose temple dominated the city skyline.

At one level it was the last place you would expect to plant a church. But Paul could see the potential of a vibrant Christian community in such a hostile environment. He committed himself to be based there for almost two years – but such a move took courage on his part and from those who would become followers of Christ.

Many of us make the mistake of thinking that courage means having no fear. But courage means facing fear as a mountain – and by God's grace learning to climb over it. Mark Twain captured it perfectly when he wrote: 'Courage is resistance to fear, mastery of fear not absence of fear'.

> ▶ Fear can dominate our lives in so many ways. Talk together about what makes you fearful. It may be long-held hidden fears or fears that are very apparent at the present moment because of your circumstances.
> ▶ As a church, are there things that you are fearful of at the moment? This could be the potential failure of a project, decreasing numbers, growing conflict and schism, loss of leadership, etc.

Let's spend some time learning in very practical ways how Paul faces fear and finds courage.

Our study reveals four helpful lessons about facing fear and finding courage.

1. Partnerships provide support (Acts 18:1–5)

When we wrestle with fear one of God's grace-gifts to help us is other people. Friends can be a wonderful means of strength when we face tough times.

Paul arrived in Corinth and met a married couple and struck up what was to become a life-long friendship. The couple were called Priscilla and Aquila and together with Paul they formed a special partnership (see Romans 16:3–4 for Paul's opinion of them).

In a remarkable series of coincidences (perhaps better described as God-incidences) the three discover they share:

▶ A common culture – Aquila and Priscilla were Jews as Paul was
▶ A common faith – they shared Paul's belief that Jesus was the Messiah
▶ A common trade – they ran a tent-making business – and that was Paul's trade too
▶ A common story – following Jesus had disrupted Paul's life and it appears to have had the same effect on Priscilla and Aquila (see box 'Riots in Rome').

Paul teamed up with Priscilla and Aquila and they shared their home with him. The three of them ran the tent-making business, which covered their overheads, and Paul used the opportunity of Sabbath worship in the synagogue to share the message about Jesus.

▶ Think back over the last few years and identify friends who have come into your own life who have become significant in the partnership/friendship that has developed.
▶ Did you share any of the following:
    A common story
    A common culture
    A common faith
    A common trade
▶ Just reflect for a moment on your church and see how you being a part of that church brings a greater richness to the Christian community that you belong to. Although you are a diverse group what are the things you have found that you have in common?

Individually we all carry with us the personal burdens of fear, but together we are stronger if we help carry burdens for each other and give each other the courage to face them.

Riots in Rome

Luke tells us that Aquila and Priscilla ended up in Corinth because they had been expelled from Rome along with all members of the Jewish community. What he writes is confirmed by the Roman historian Suetonius, who offers an explanation as to why this happened.

Suetonius pinpoints the date of Emperor Claudius' decree as AD 49 and explains that public riots had broken out within the Jewish community in Rome. The emperor ordered an immediate crackdown – all Jews were to leave and take their disputes elsewhere; the capital of the Roman Empire would not be disrupted in this way. Suetonius even gives a clue to the cause of the riots – they took place 'at the instigation of Chrestus'. This has led some to suggest that *Chrestus* could mean *Christos* or *Christ*.

Perhaps the riots were caused because Jews – such as Aquila and Priscilla – had believed the message that Jesus was the long-awaited Messiah and this caused offence to the Jewish establishment in Rome.

We don't know for certain, but we can see that God used this couple in exile, however long it lasted. We are also reminded that God's purposes are not derailed by political events.

When Paul's team members, Silas and Timothy, arrive (18:5) he is able to go full time with his ministry of preaching and teaching about Jesus. The suggestion is that his team members worked to release Paul to do what he did best. They got on – initially at least – with tent-making and making sure there was food to eat and a bed to sleep in.

It's interesting to note here that Paul's role changed when others arrived. Sometimes we need to let go of roles we have had for some time. Good teams release people to develop. Paul, Silas and Timothy all changed in their roles as their journeys continued together.

▶ What are your roles in the church or at work or in the family?
▶ Have these roles changed over the years? Talk about the importance of the teams around you that have given you the courage to take on a new role.

When Paul faced the challenge of Corinth, the Lord provided some partners to share the load.

Often when we lack courage God brings strength through friends and partners

– and the best ones are those whose care is practical and down to earth. That is why it is wise to invest in such relationships for there will be times when we can offer support and other occasions when we can receive it as well. We all need strong supportive friendships as we seek to follow Christ.

> ▶ Talk about your small group in terms of how you support one another. Is it a group with whom you feel you can be yourself and how is that achieved?
> ▶ What ways does your church invest in supportive friendships? What are you doing in your church that is helping you gain strong supportive friendships as you seek to follow Christ?
> ▶ Churches are not theatres where you book your weekly ticket for the Sunday performance but sometimes we need to have space to be. Does your church give you appropriate space to breathe as well as a place to be busy?

2. Strategy provides a framework (Acts 18:6–8)

Another grace-gift to help us at times of fear is be sure we are treading a Holy Spirit directed course. God-given plans help us to remain focussed on the goal when fear and insecurity loom large.

Paul had a method he usually followed. He would find the local Jewish community and give his attention to them until they refused to listen. At that point he would turn to the non-Jewish segment of the population and concentrate on them.

He followed this pattern in Corinth but when the abuse started (18:6) Paul shook out his clothes as a prophetic enactment and set up camp in the house right next door to the synagogue which was conveniently located but perhaps not the most tactful of moves! (18:7) The leader of the Jewish community – Crispus – was converted and baptised as a follower of Jesus, together with his whole family. Like a snowball rolling down hill, Crispus' story helped spread the message about Jesus. The whole thing gathered momentum and soon many others were converted.

Paul stuck with what he knew would work. There is nothing unspiritual in planning and organising provided it is done in faith and with prayer. The old adage is true: 'Those who aim at nothing hit it every time'.

When we face pressure the temptation is to panic and abandon our course – but the lesson we learn from Paul in Corinth is to stick to the plan and trust God for the outcome.

- Are you somebody who likes to have a strategy in your life? Or are you somebody who likes a sense of open space to allow opportunity to come your way?
- How can the church capture both these characteristics: planning and organising the vision and life of the church while still enabling the church to plan and trust God for the outcome?
- Is there a place for strategic thinkers to use their gifts? Are they encouraged to build and work as a team rather than individuals?

3. Strength to face our fears (Acts 18:9-11)

Paul wrestled with deep fear and insecurity during his opening weeks in Corinth. We know that for two reasons. First, Luke recounts a powerful experience where the Lord Jesus appeared to Paul in a vision and reassured him (18:9-11). Secondly, we have Paul's own testimony where he makes a frank admission about how he felt when he arrived in Corinth 'in weakness and fear and with much trembling' (1 Cor. 2:3).

The picture of Paul in the Bible suggests he was a strong even forceful person who had no hesitation in standing up for what he believed to be right. Somehow the idea of him being terrified doesn't seem to fit. But the Bible never places people on pedestals – that is our weakness. And Paul is not reluctant about sharing his vulnerability – he discovered that openness about weakness led to an outpouring of divine strength (2 Cor. 12:10).

We are faced with a question: what was it about Corinth that filled Paul with fear? We can only speculate but perhaps his anxieties stemmed from a variety of things.

Spiritually Corinth was a dark place
Paul was aware of the spiritual battle (Eph. 6:10-13) and Corinth was a city that manifested a strong presence of evil forces.

Emotionally Paul may have feared rejection
Some have suggested that the ridicule he received at Athens may have come at a low point in Paul's life. He travelled to Corinth low in his spirits and this gave rise to his feelings of fear.

Physically Paul was scarred
It was only a matter of weeks since Paul had endured a vicious flogging which had left wounds that were still in the process of healing. The prospect of another riot and physical attack would fill anyone with fear.

Whatever the cause, Paul's feelings of fear were real – he *trembled*.

> ▶ Take a moment to think back to the things that make you fearful. Like Paul
> we can suffer real fear – so much so that we can tremble. Like Paul we can
> receive real encouragement and strength from God.
> ▶ How did this happen for Paul and how has it happened for you?

Paul's testimony as recorded by Luke tells of the Lord Jesus speaking directly to him
one night in a vision. The Lord's words of encouragement went to the heart of Paul's
anxieties.

'Do not be afraid; keep on speaking, do not be silent. For I am with you and no-one
is going to attack and harm you because I have many people in this city.' (18:9–10)

This message must have come to Paul like water in the desert. The Lord addressed
the root of his fears and assured him that he was in the right place and that there
was a job for him to do. His welfare was in the hands of Jesus so Paul could
concentrate on his work knowing that there were many people in Corinth whose
hearts had been prepared by the Lord.

Paul believed what he heard and made the decision to stay put and get on with the
task of sharing the good news about Jesus (18:11).

In one of his New Testament letters Paul tells another church, 'I can do everything
through him who gives me strength' (Phil. 4:13). For Paul that was not a nice theory
but something he had proved to be true – even in a tough place such as Corinth.

> ▶ Look at Paul's response to what God said to him.
>   He heard God's words of assurance
>   He believed and trusted God
>   He decided to get on with his task
> ▶ Talk together about how we can respond in the same way to God's
> reassurance to us.

4. Conflict is to be expected (Acts 18:12–17)
An important lesson for all of us to learn and remember is that in the Christian life,
pressure is normal.

At first reading, this section of Luke's report seems less than essential to the story
of Corinth. Why did he include the abortive case brought against Paul before the
Roman Proconsul (or governor) Gallio?

Probably Luke's motive was to demonstrate that here was one of a number of public officials who chose not to see Christianity as a threat to the empire. Gallio's decision could be seen as setting a legal precedent that others who relied on Luke's 'orderly account' (Luke 1:1–4; Acts 1:1–2) might wish to cite if they found themselves in legal hot water.

But the incident serves as a reminder that although the case against Paul was thrown out, his ministry in Corinth did attract opposition. It is impossible to read the book of Acts without drawing the conclusion that conflict is par for the course for followers of Christ. It may take various forms from outright persecution through to cynical disregard. As Paul told his young colleague Timothy, 'In fact everyone who wants to live a godly life in Christ Jesus will be persecuted' (2 Tim. 3:12).

The unfortunate Sosthenes who received a beating from his angry congregation (18:17) may possibly be the same man Paul refers to in his first letter to the church in Corinth (1 Cor. 1:1). We cannot be certain about this but if it is the same Sosthenes he would be the second chair of the synagogue to be converted (18:8) which reveals something of the impact of the gospel on this community. It seems the Lord really did have 'many people in this city'.

SUMMING UP
Paul's experience in finding God's grace to overcome fear at Corinth reminds us of four principles:

▶ Partnership – we need to cultivate strong relationships
▶ Strategy – plans give us focus when fear threatens
▶ Strength – God's strength is always available
▶ Conflict – pressure is par for the course for a Christian

Maurice Chevalier, the legendary entertainer, suffered a breakdown at the height of his career and feared he would never perform in public again. An elderly doctor served as his counsellor during this dark time. He invited Chevalier to sing at a country fair when only a couple of hundred people would be present. He suggested this would be a test of his recovery. Chevalier declined and said he feared he would never perform in public again. The elderly doctor told him, 'Maurice, don't be afraid to be afraid'. Chevalier later wrote that this was the turning point in his recovery process. He was waiting for the perfect moment when fear would be gone for ever. He discovered that would never happen. Fear had to be clearly identified – and then faced.

Paul faced his fears at Corinth and found that the strength of the Lord Jesus was able to carry him through the challenges he faced.

And we can discover that same strength to help us face our fears as well.

DURING THE WEEK

During this coming week what would you want God to say to you in your situation?

> *"Do not be afraid*
> *Keep on ....*
> *Do not ....*
> *For I am with you*
> *And no-one/nothing is going to ...."*

PRAYER

'Don't be afraid to be afraid'. Spend some time bringing your fears to God and listening to his response to you.

Ask someone to read Psalm 27 or read it together with time to be still and quiet.

Help one another to take courage remembering, 'Courage is resistance to fear, mastery of fear not absence of fear'.

PEOPLE OF FAITH

AIM:To learn, share and experience the full message of the gospel

READ Acts 19:1–20

While Apollos was at Corinth, Paul took the road through the interior and arrived at Ephesus. There he found some disciples and asked them, "Did you receive the Holy Spirit when you believed?"

They answered, "No, we have not even heard that there is a Holy Spirit."

So Paul asked, "Then what baptism did you receive?"

"John's baptism," they replied.

Paul said, "John's baptism was a baptism of repentance. He told the people to believe in the one coming after him, that is, in Jesus." On hearing this, they were baptised into the name of the Lord Jesus. When Paul placed his hands on them, the Holy Spirit came on them, and they spoke in tongues and prophesied. There were about twelve men in all.

Paul entered the synagogue and spoke boldly there for three months, arguing persuasively about the kingdom of God. But some of them became obstinate; they refused to believe and publicly maligned the Way. So Paul left them. He took the disciples with him and had discussions daily in the lecture hall of Tyrannus. This went on for two years, so that all the Jews and Greeks who lived in the province of Asia heard the word of the Lord.

God did extraordinary miracles through Paul, so that even handkerchiefs and aprons that had touched him were taken to the sick, and their illnesses were cured and the evil spirits left them.

Some Jews who went around driving out evil spirits tried to invoke the name of the Lord Jesus over those who were demon-possessed. They would say, "In the name of Jesus, whom Paul preaches, I command you to come out." Seven sons of Sceva, a Jewish chief priest, were doing this. One day the evil spirit answered them, "Jesus I know, and I know about Paul, but who are you?" Then the man who had the evil spirit jumped on them and overpowered them all. He gave them such a beating that they ran out of the house naked and bleeding.

When this became known to the Jews and Greeks living in Ephesus, they were all seized with fear, and the name of the Lord Jesus was held in high honour. Many of those who believed now came and openly confessed their evil deeds. A number who had practised sorcery brought their scrolls together and burned them publicly. When they calculated the value of the scrolls, the total came to fifty thousand drachmas. In this way the word of the Lord spread widely and grew in power.

TO SET THE SCENE

A small boy in Sunday School was asked to define faith.

'Faith is believing things you know aren't true,' he replied. Sadly, his answer is close to what some people believe.

> ▶ What do you think people put their faith in today?
> ▶ To what extent can these things be trusted or will they let you down?

The Bible offers a more accurate definition of faith, 'Now faith is being sure of what we hope for and certain of what we do not see' (Heb. 11:1).

> ▶ Taking this definition of faith from Hebrews how is it different from the other things that we can be tempted to put our faith in?
> ▶ Why is the Christian faith as described in Hebrews difficult at times? How can we be sure when we can't see?

Having talked together about this thing called 'faith', Paul's adventures in Ephesus help us to explore what it means to be people of faith and how we are called to help pass that faith on to others.

Our study takes us to the busy sea-port of Ephesus – a city Paul had visited before with his friends in ministry, Aquila and Priscilla. Paul had been invited to stay longer but had other plans. So he had promised to return for a longer visit one day if the Lord made it possible (Acts 18:19–21).

Paul could see that Ephesus was a key city in the world of his day. He saw it as an ideal place to base himself and work effectively for two years.

INTRODUCING EPHESUS

Ephesus was an important city in the 1st century world. Here are some key facts that explain something of the city's significance.

It was the market place of Asia Minor
Ephesus was the busiest harbour in Asia and stood at the mouth of the Cayster River and the Aegean Sea. Three major trade routes converged there making it the gateway to the Province of Asia Minor.

It was an Assize town
The Roman Governor would visit regularly and hear legal cases and much status, colour, pomp and pageantry was associated with this.

It was home to the Pan-Ionian Games
This athletics contest was held annually in May when thousands would attend to spectate or participate.

It was a great religious centre
Ephesus was home to one of the Seven Wonders of the Ancient World. The Temple of Artemis was dedicated to Artemis the goddess of the Ephesians – or Diana to give her Latin name. This was an impressive building measuring 425' long x 220' wide x 60' high.

It was supported by 120 columns each donated by a king and 36 of the columns were richly covered with gold and jewels. Its centrepiece was a statue of the goddess they believed had fallen from heaven. People came to visit the temple and worship. It was a fertility cult – so worship involved having sex with a temple prostitute – and hundreds of women were employed for that purpose.

It was a haven for criminals
A tradition existed that offered freedom and immunity from prosecution to any who stayed within the Temple precincts actually defined as a bowshot.

The result was it became the centre for organised crime as it attracted a host of unsavoury characters who were lived there.

It was a centre for pagan superstition
Ephesus was a city where the occult, magic and the dark arts flourished. It was booming business – you could buy amulets, charms, so-called 'Ephesian Letters' that would promise help if you were childless, needed luck in business, safety in travel and a host of other things.

Paul made his return visit in due course and ended up staying in Ephesus for two fruitful years during which time many people became followers of Jesus.

As we follow Luke's summary of this period we discover three things which will build people of faith.

- Teaching – learning the faith
- Evangelism – sharing the faith
- Power – experiencing the faith

1. The need for teaching (Acts 19:1-7)

On returning to Ephesus Paul met a group of men – about twelve in number – who had a confused view about the message of Jesus. They had only understood part of the message – the bit that had been entrusted to John the Baptist (Matt. 3:1-12) concerning the need for people to turn from their sins and get ready for God's Messiah.

As Paul questioned these men he discovered they had not received the Holy Spirit or even understood that he existed. Paul lost no time in filling in the gaps in their understanding as he explained the message of God's love as shown in the death and resurrection of Jesus Christ. This concluded with the men being baptised in water in the name of Jesus as an outward sign of their commitment. Luke records that as Paul laid hands on them and prayed they received the gift of the Holy Spirit (19:6).

> - If appropriate take a moment to ask if anyone has any questions about the work of the Holy Spirit in our lives as Christians. We will look at this aspect of the Christian life in greater detail in session 6.

These men had only heard part of the story and needed someone to explain it clearly in language they could understand. We are reminded of the need to teach the message about Christ that exists in every generation. Throughout our church programme and across all age groups we need to be committed to teaching the faith taking nothing for granted about those who listen.

> - Pause for a moment and identify the many ways that the Christian message of good news is taught across all the age groups. Be encouraged by what you talk about and maybe be aware of any gaps that become apparent.

Like Paul's friends in Ephesus, there are people in our communities who have a confused view about the faith. They have only understood half of the story and are left with a stack of unanswered questions. The value of courses like Alpha and

Christianity Explored is that they encourage people to ask their questions and look at the basics of belief.

A teacher told her class of Year 7 children the Christmas story. One of the children remained behind with a question. 'Miss, I enjoyed the story,' the boy began, 'but there is one thing I don't understand – why did they give the baby a swear word for a name?'

Teaching the faith remains a priority for the people of God.

> ▶ Where did you first find out about the faith? Who were the significant people who taught you about the faith?
> ▶ It was during a conversation that Paul realised that these men had only picked up part of the Christian message of good news. We usually don't learn everything straightaway but need to keep learning. How does your church enable you to keep learning?
> ▶ What sort of conversations help the leadership of your church discover what needs teaching and learning?

2. The importance of evangelism (Acts 19:8-10)
Evangelism is one of those words that Christians often use but rarely define. It simply means explaining the good news about Jesus. Paul's approach in Ephesus offers some valuable lessons in telling that good news in a society that often doesn't want to listen.

We should expect opposition
Paul seized a twelve-week window of opportunity as he embarked on his customary method of beginning with the Jewish community. The synagogue congregation provided a ready audience who knew the Old Testament scriptures. The Jews shared an eager longing for the coming of God's anointed one (or Messiah) and Paul used the open worship format of the synagogue to explain how these prophecies had been fulfilled in Jesus of Nazareth.

Luke reports that Paul 'spoke boldly' as he engaged in 'arguing persuasively about the kingdom of God' (19:8). But after three months the good will ran out and some in the Jewish community began to abuse Paul and publicly malign Jesus.

Sometimes we are paralysed by the fear that people will stop liking us if we appear too keen about our faith in Christ. Such a fear can hold us back from the task of sharing our faith with sensitivity and understanding. It seems that Paul expected opportunity and opposition to go hand in hand (see his comments on his work in Ephesus in 1 Corinthians 16:8–9).

Abraham Lincoln famously stated that 'you can't please all of the people all of the time' and that is especially true when it comes to living as a follower of Christ.

Opposition to the message about Jesus takes different forms – but it will always rear its head somewhere whenever people begin to talk about him and the difference he can make.

> ▶ Paul expected opposition when he began to talk about his faith. Do we expect opposition? Or do we expect to be ignored or classified as 'odd' and end up just not talking about our faith?
> ▶ Do you know of someone who can talk about their faith in a very easy manner? What is it that makes them easy to listen to and easy to talk to?

We need to be creative
The opposition his efforts stirred up did not deter Paul – instead he made a bold and creative move. He hired a secular lecture hall belonging to a man called Tyrannus (19:9). Some older manuscripts of the New Testament add the information that Paul did this between the hours of 11 am and 4 pm – the hottest part of the day. Tyrannus and his students dropped lectures during these hot hours so Paul seized the opportunity to offer something for the many visitors passing through Ephesus.

Too often our evangelism is locked into predictable patterns and much of it is held within the limitations of church premises. We need to be bold and imaginative in discovering new ways of connecting with people and helping them discover God's transforming love.

Think about the creative flow that has inspired the people of God over the centuries:

▶ Wesley and Whitfield both used open air preaching
▶ William Booth and his 'salvation army' and lively music
▶ Billy Graham and his use of massive sports stadiums

- Why do we think that innovation and creativity are friends when looking back yet enemies in the present?
- How is your church creating new ways of teaching the faith in bold and imaginative ways?
- Paul had to do his groundwork to get to know Tyrannus, creating the possibility of holding lectures at a time and in a place where it would work for those who wanted to come. Then he stuck with it. What groundwork do we need to undertake with local people and organisations to find new ways of teaching the faith?
- What new ways can your church teach the faith to people who have not come into contact with the Christian faith before but want to learn?

We are called to be persistent

Paul kept up his daily meetings for two years and Luke adds this remarkable comment, 'so that all the Jews and Greeks who lived in the province of Asia heard the word of the Lord' (19:10).

Luke identified the strategic importance of Paul's decision to base himself in Ephesus for this two-year period. Ephesus was a gateway city into a region then called Asia Minor. People travelled through the city because boats from all over the known world called in there to deposit cargo and passengers. Paul realised that by raising the profile of the gospel there he could be more effective than if he took to the road for two years.

But perhaps the most important thing to note is his persistence – he stuck at his task for two solid years. With so much in our culture being short term and temporary we are reminded that when it comes to evangelism, the best fruit takes time to grow.

3. The necessity of power (Acts 19:11–20)

Luke records the impact of Paul's work among the people of Ephesus. He chooses the word 'extraordinary' (19:11) to describe some of the miracles that took place presumably to make the distinction with ordinary ones!

We find it hard to take in what was happening; people were getting hold of the sweat bands and aprons Paul used in his tent-making work and taking them to people who were sick and they were being healed.

Luke also relates the story of the men who tried to use the name of Jesus and were badly beaten up by a demonised man.

Luke records these unusual incidents to make an important point: 'When this became known to the Jews and Greeks living in Ephesus, they were all seized with fear and the name of the Lord Jesus was held in high honour' (19:17). A remarkable God-awareness came on the people of Ephesus and the name of Jesus was held in high regard because of the demonstrations of power they witnessed.

Ephesus was a city rife with superstitions and occult practices. Luke reports that many of those who decided to follow Jesus Christ brought their scrolls and charms to a massive public bonfire. Almost as an aside Luke records the value of those things that were burned – by current standards this would amount to two million pounds.

The impact of the gospel in Ephesus was considerable (19:20) and people in the city and surrounding region came to a personal encounter with the living God through his Son Jesus Christ. Reading further in Luke's narrative (19:23–41) we learn of an economic downturn among the sale of images because of the impact of Paul's ministry. A trade union meeting erupted into a near riot because of the influence of the message of Jesus on people who turned from superstitions and false beliefs.

We cannot manufacture such power encounters nor should we try to talk things up by exaggerated claims. But we should look for lives that are changed for good by the power of God. That should be a focus for our prayers as we share the good news among our friends. Paul sums this up concisely in one of his letters when he wrote:

'For the Kingdom of God is not a matter of talk but of power.' (1 Cor. 4:20)

SUMMING UP
The call to be people of faith extends beyond just believing certain things. In the New Testament *belief, behaviour* and *belonging* are all linked together for those who are followers of Christ.

Believing – reminds us of the core elements of the gospel that explain the good news.

Belonging – reminds us that we are called to be part of the believing community of Christ's followers, his church.

Behaving – reminds us of the call to live lives that are worthy of this good news.

And part of that call is seeking to do all we can to help others find faith in Jesus too.

- Share with the group your journey of faith. Maybe you *belonged* to the church from infancy, *behaved* in the way that was expected of you but only fully *believed* in middle age. Or maybe you came to *belief* in Jesus through going to an Alpha course but found it difficult to *belong* to a church because you were expected to *behave* in a particular way.
- How do we as church members welcome newcomers who do not behave as we would expect?

DURING THE WEEK

Think about ways in which you can nurture your faith and encourage your fellow Christians to become lifelong disciples. What strategies does your church have in place to nurture long-term learning? It may be to encourage the use of Bible reading notes, reading groups, small groups, sermon series, discussion groups, organised structured courses. Think about whether any of the above would help you or someone you know.

PRAYER

Take a moment to identify long-term projects that are part of the evangelistic life of your church – telling the good news! And pray about them realising that they need your long-term commitment particularly in prayer. Pray for those involved and any other needs that you are aware of.

If you could dream of changes happening in your community that were due to the impact of the gospel, what would they be? Then pray that what you have talked about will be taken by God and turned through your willingness and faith into a demonstration of God's power.

PEOPLE OF COMMITMENT

AIM: To see the essential need to work together in making Jesus known

READ Acts 16:6–40

Paul and his companions travelled throughout the region of Phrygia and Galatia, having been kept by the Holy Spirit from preaching the word in the province of Asia. When they came to the border of Mysia, they tried to enter Bithynia, but the Spirit of Jesus would not allow them to. So they passed by Mysia and went down to Troas. During the night Paul had a vision of a man of Macedonia standing and begging him, "Come over to Macedonia and help us." After Paul had seen the vision, we got ready at once to leave for Macedonia, concluding that God had called us to preach the gospel to them.

From Troas we put out to sea and sailed straight for Samothrace, and the next day on to Neapolis. From there we travelled to Philippi, a Roman colony and the leading city of that district of Macedonia. And we stayed there several days.

On the Sabbath we went outside the city gate to the river, where we expected to find a place of prayer. We sat down and began to speak to the women who had gathered there. One of those listening was a woman named Lydia, a dealer in purple cloth from the city of Thyatira, who was a worshipper of God. The Lord opened her heart to respond to Paul's message. When she and the members of her household were baptised, she invited us to her home. "If you consider me a believer in the Lord," she said, "come and stay at my house." And she persuaded us.

Once when we were going to the place of prayer, we were met by a slave girl who had a spirit by which she predicted the future. She earned a great deal of money for her owners by fortune-telling. This girl followed Paul and the rest of us, shouting, "These men are servants of the Most High God, who are telling you the way to be saved." She kept this up for many days. Finally Paul became so troubled that he turned round and said to the spirit, "In the name of Jesus Christ I command you to come out of her!" At that moment the spirit left her.

When the owners of the slave girl realised that their hope of making money was gone, they seized Paul and Silas and dragged them into the market-place to face the authorities. They brought them before the magistrates and said, "These men are Jews, and are throwing our city into an uproar by advocating customs unlawful for us Romans to accept or practise."

The crowd joined in the attack against Paul and Silas, and the magistrates ordered them to be stripped and beaten. After they had been severely flogged, they were thrown into prison, and the jailer was commanded to guard them carefully. Upon receiving such orders, he put them in the inner cell and fastened their feet in the stocks.

About midnight Paul and Silas were praying and singing hymns to God, and the other prisoners were listening to them. Suddenly there was such a violent earthquake that the foundations of the prison were shaken. At once all the prison doors flew open, and everybody's chains came loose. The jailer woke up, and when he saw the prison doors open, he drew his sword and was about to kill himself because he thought the prisoners had escaped. But Paul shouted, "Don't harm yourself! We are all here!"

The jailer called for lights, rushed in and fell trembling before Paul and Silas. He then brought them out and asked, "Sirs, what must I do to be saved?"

They replied, "Believe in the Lord Jesus, and you will be saved—you and your household." Then they spoke the word of the Lord to him and to all the others in his house. At that hour of the night the jailer took them and washed their wounds; then immediately he and all his family were baptised. The jailer brought them into his house and set a meal before them; he was filled with joy because he had come to believe in God—he and his whole family.

When it was daylight, the magistrates sent their officers to the jailer with the order: "Release those men." The jailer told Paul, "The magistrates have ordered that you and Silas be released. Now you can leave. Go in peace."

But Paul said to the officers: "They beat us publicly without a trial, even though we are Roman citizens, and threw us into prison. And now do they want to get rid of us quietly? No! Let them come themselves and escort us out."

The officers reported this to the magistrates, and when they heard that Paul and Silas were Roman citizens, they were alarmed. They came to appease them and escorted them from the prison, requesting them to leave the city. After Paul and Silas came out of the prison, they went to Lydia's house, where they met with the brothers and encouraged them. Then they left.

TO SET THE SCENE

It's exciting to trace your roots. Some people go to great lengths to draw their family tree and track down relatives on the other side of the world. Our study tells the remarkable story behind the planting of the first church on European soil. As far as we know, the congregation established by Paul in Philippi marked the coming of the gospel to the continent of Europe.

Whatever the label on the building where we meet to worship, those of us who are European Christians trace our roots back to Acts 16. And as we look at our heritage we discover what it means to live as people of commitment.

> ▶ As we begin this study together take a moment to find out how long the members of the group have been part of the your church. Who has been around the longest? What churches have you attended before being part of the present one? Consider, even in your small group, the glimpses of a world church with a great heritage.

Paul and his ministry team reveal the characteristics of people of commitment:

- ▶ They were *focussed*
- ▶ They were *directed*
- ▶ They were *united*
- ▶ They were *dedicated*

1. They were focussed (Acts 16:6)

Paul and his colleagues had a clear aim as they travelled through the Roman Empire. Luke summarises this aim as 'preaching the word' (16:6)which is one of several shorthand descriptions he uses in Acts to describe the mission of making Jesus known. Michael Green sums up that clear mission of the first followers of Jesus:

> *Without clarity of aim, one achieves nothing. These men and women had great clarity of aim: they wanted to see people from every background in antiquity won to the exclusive allegiance of Jesus Christ.*
>
> *Acts for Today*, Michael Green (Hodder and Stoughton, 1993, p69)

The good news was brought to Europe by a group of people with a clear desire to make Jesus known. They were not on some kind of sightseeing tour fuelled by idle curiosity – their vision went beyond personal pleasure in order to reach people who had yet to hear of Christ.

It has become popular in recent years for churches to draw up mission statements, which are an attempt to put into words their reason for existence. From what we read in the New Testament we could summarise the mission statement of the first Christians with the phrase: 'To make Jesus Christ known'.

▶ How does that phrase translate
in your every day life
in the mission and life of your church?

The success of any enterprise is determined by the ability of those involved to answer three basic questions;

Where are we from?
Why are we here?
Where are we going?

Although we are always asking these questions and always answering them, as a church we need a sense of where we have come from and what has brought us individually and corporately to this moment in time, so that we can have a unified commitment to where we are going. Paul and his team could answer these questions as they had a clear focus for their mission.

2. They were directed (Acts 16:6-10)
Even people who have a strong focus can experience struggles over guidance.

These verses reveal something of the confusion Paul and his mission team experienced as they tried to discover what was on God's agenda at this particular time. The verses only give part of the story and we are left guessing as to the details of what went on. What Luke summarises in a few sentences may well have covered a period of weeks or months. Guidance rarely drops from the sky and can often be a testing period of waiting.

What is clear is that Paul and his friends found their plans frustrated not once but twice. The Holy Spirit prevented them from entering Asia (16:6) and their attempt to travel to Bithynia was halted because 'the Spirit of Jesus would not allow them to' (16:7). We are not told how the Lord closed both of these doors but the team travelled to the coastal city of Troas probably feeling despondent and confused. While staying there Paul had a vivid vision of a man pleading intensely for him to come and help. Paul recognised the man as a native of Macedonia and he and his team concluded that this was God's call for the next phase of their work.

Paul knew what it was to have plans and yet to see those plans frustrated.

> ▶ In your own lives and/or in the life of your church, when have you felt that
> something was right and thought that God had guided you only to find those
> plans frustrated?
> ▶ What can we learn from Paul and his plans in Acts 16 in terms of timing,
> waiting and persisting?

In fact, this change of direction was to occupy Paul for the next seven or eight years
so it was a life-changing event (the details are covered by Luke in Acts 15:36–18:18;
18:23–21:16). This significant phase of Paul's life is sometimes referred to as his
Aegean Mission because it concentrated on the coastline around the Aegean Sea
– which nowadays we tend to associate with holidays in the sun rather than the
back-breaking work of church planting.

The lesson for us here is clear. Paul and his friends were not working to their own
blueprint - they were directed by the Lord at every stage of their mission. It is never
enough to simply have enthusiasm and a bunch of good ideas. Even calling those
ideas a vision in the hope that using so-called spiritual language will make them
acceptable doesn't work. The gospel came to Europe because a group of Christians
were open to the leading of the Lord – even if that involved their own preferences
being set on one side. We can learn much from their example.

> ▶ Guidance comes to those who admit they need to be guided, rather than
> relying on their own wisdom. How can you encourage one another to be
> open to God's leading and guiding Spirit even if it involves putting your own
> preferences to one side?

3. They were united (Acts 16:6)

The account given by Luke makes it clear that Paul was not engaged in a solo
enterprise. It was very much a case of team work: 'Paul and his companions
travelled'(16:6). Notice also how often the word 'we' occurs from verse 10 onwards.
This is the first of several passages in Acts where Luke joined the team and takes
the role of an eyewitness reporter.

As well as Luke, Timothy and Silas accompanied Paul and probably there
were others who are not named. This apostolic team shared the load as they
worked together with Paul as the leader. But team ministry was not without its
complications as Paul and Barnabas discovered to their cost (see Acts 15:36–41).

It would be easy to misread the story of the church plant in Philippi as the heroic
endeavours of one man – Paul. But the bulk of his work involved others and that is
the pattern by which kingdom work gets done. For a local church to grow healthy

and strong it needs a strong sense of team. If we rely on one gifted leader then we limit the extent of growth. Luke's account of the rather difficult process of discovering God's direction has a sense of collective teamwork behind the decision: 'After Paul had seen the vision, we got ready at once to leave for Macedonia, concluding that God had called us to preach the gospel to them' (16:10).

As we read on in Acts we discover the team faced some tough times ahead. More than once they would prove the value of standing together in the mission of making Christ known.

▶ What teams can you identify in your church and which ones are you a part of?
▶ Is teamwork encouraged in your church or is power centrally held?
▶ What can be done to encourage every member membership and increased commitment in the mission and life of your church?

Read the Synergy piece below. Then spend time to laugh! Have you ever felt isolated like that? Or do you identify with those who are distracted and unable to commit fully.

4. They were dedicated (Acts 16:13-40)
The next section reads as an amazing mission adventure but see how this mission in Philippi developed in three stages according to Luke.

Stage 1 Lydia and her friends (Acts 16:13-15)
Philippi didn't have a large enough Jewish community to run a synagogue but on the Sabbath Paul and his team found the next best thing - a place of prayer by the River Gangites where a group of women had gathered. One of them was a merchant business woman named Lydia from the city of Thyatira. Luke records that the Lord opened her heart to Paul's message about Jesus and she and members of her household were baptised. Lydia was obviously a woman of some wealth and she opened her home to the team as a base for them in Philippi.

Such a positive early response to their message must have boosted Paul and his team but some stormy weather lay ahead.

▶ Share the name of somebody or some event that in the last few weeks has been a source of encouragement to you or your church.

Stage 2 An abused slave girl (Acts 16:16-24)
It is hard to comprehend the miserable life this anonymous slave girl endured at the hands of her unscrupulous owners. She was demonised and the men who owned her used her as a fortune teller but when she saw Paul and his team she identified

SYNERGY

Synergy is a word that describes the working together of several drugs or muscles to produce an effect greater than the sum of their individual parts.

The principle is true in local church life – we can achieve more by working together than by doing our own thing.

That principle is the opposite of what appeared in one church magazine:

> *There are 560 members in our church*
> *But 100 and frail and elderly*
> *That leaves 460 to do the work*
> *But 74 are young people away at college*
> *That leaves 386 to do all the work*
> *But 150 are tired because of work commitments*
> *So that leaves 236 to do all the work*
> *And 150 are mums with small children*
> *That leaves 86*
> *A further 46 have important interests*
> *That leaves 40 to do all the work*
> *But 15 live too far away to come regularly*
> *So that leaves 25 to do all the work*
> *And 23 say they've done their bit*
> *So that leaves you and me*
> *And I'm shattered*
> *So the best of luck to you!*

them as the servants of the most high God who had a message about finding salvation. Luke reveals that this went on for a long time (16:18) and it obviously caused some concern to the team. Eventually Paul brings release to this troubled girl by calling on the all-powerful name of Jesus.

But such an act of mercy is met with fury by the men who used and abused the girl – they were more concerned with their loss of income than her finding freedom.

Paul and Silas (we are not told where the rest of the team were on this particular day) were dragged before the city magistrates who ordered them to be publicly stripped and flogged. At the conclusion of this humiliating and painful ordeal they were thrown in the city jail and fastened in stocks leaving their bruised bodies not even the slightest chance of respite.

Stage 3 A miracle at midnight (Acts 16:25-40)

In spite of their pain, Paul and Silas were engaged in a worship service in the most unlikely surroundings – and their fellow prisoners proved to be an eager audience (16:25). Suddenly an earthquake hits the city jail causing doors and chains to come loose. The jailer – convinced he had lost his prisoners – opted for suicide rather than face the awful consequences of losing his charges. But Paul stopped him in the nick of time and the terrified man pleaded for help. His question' 'What must I do to be saved?' (16:30) probably had more to do with his concern for his skin than his soul. The extraordinary episode ends with Paul and Silas receiving much needed medical treatment, having a meal with the jailer's family, sharing the gospel with them and baptising them in the name of Jesus.

The following morning the magistrates issue the order for Paul and Silas to be released but Paul draws on his right as a Roman citizen to receive a fair trial. The magistrates are horrified to learn that in the heat of the moment they had not even checked. Such a mistake could render them liable to punishment themselves. Paul's insistence that they should come and personally escort him out of jail was probably more to do with his desire to buy some time and peace for the fledgling church than a personal fit of pique. That small congregation seems to have been based at Lydia's house (16:40).

Luke only recorded the main highlights of the visit to Philippi – but we get the picture. This church was born at great personal cost to Paul and his team. Their dedication forged some special, rich relationships that are reflected in a letter Paul wrote to the church years later (Phil. 1:3-11). Fire usually forges indestructible friendships.

> ▶ As we look at our own role within our local church we are faced with a challenging question: am I really committed to serve Christ here – or just loosely involved?

SUMMING UP

As we trace the roots of the first church in Europe we have seen the commitment of the missionary team. They had a clear focus, were open to the direction of the Holy Spirit and worked as a team with great dedication. There they faced strong opposition – and saw lasting fruit.

Someone once described the difference between involvement and commitment as being like bacon and eggs for breakfast. The chicken was involved – but the pig was committed.

DURING THE WEEK

As a group commit to praying for one another and your church in the coming week. Are there specific situations where members of your group are praying for guidance? Commit to praying for that specific situation during the week.

PRAYER

Pray for those you know at home or abroad who are 'going through the fire' at great personal cost. Pray that they may be given indestructible friendships to support and sustain them in their time of need.

Going

Strong, pure, bright and near,
clear is the voice I have heard.
My confidence rests in the proof of your love,
my hope in the truth of your word.

I was made for the praise of your glory,
I was formed for the purpose you planned:
each moment I live
is the gift that you give
and my future is held in your hand.

I was saved by your infinite mercy,
I have wealth more than any could earn:
you gave up your breath
to redeem me from death
and I give all I am in return.

I will follow wherever you lead me,
I will know that your promise is true:
I will fix on the grace
Of your beckoning face,
I will walk
on the water
with you.

The Sky is your Oyster, Mike Hollow (Monarch, 2003, p 133)

PEOPLE OF PROMISE

AIM: To be challenged afresh by the abiding significance of Pentecost

READ Acts 2:1-13

When the day of Pentecost came, they were all together in one place. Suddenly a sound like the blowing of a violent wind came from heaven and filled the whole house where they were sitting. They saw what seemed to be tongues of fire that separated and came to rest on each of them. All of them were filled with the Holy Spirit and began to speak in other tongues as the Spirit enabled them.

Now there were staying in Jerusalem God-fearing Jews from every nation under heaven. When they heard this sound, a crowd came together in bewilderment, because each one heard them speaking in his own language. Utterly amazed, they asked: "Are not all these men who are speaking Galileans? Then how is it that each of us hears them in his own native language? Parthians, Medes and Elamites; residents of Mesopotamia, Judea and Cappadocia, Pontus and Asia, Phrygia and Pamphylia, Egypt and the parts of Libya near Cyrene; visitors from Rome (both Jews and converts to Judaism); Cretans and Arabs— we hear them declaring the wonders of God in our own tongues!" Amazed and perplexed, they asked one another, "What does this mean?"

Some, however, made fun of them and said, "They have had too much wine."

TO SET THE SCENE

We often talk about promising people in terms of their potential – 'She is a promising athlete' or 'He is a promising musician'. But our study about Christ's followers as people of promise refers not so much to our potential as to the outworking of Jesus' promise to all who follow him. Before he returned to heaven, Jesus gave his disciples strict instructions to stay in Jerusalem until they had an encounter with the Holy Spirit that Jesus described in terms of baptism – being covered from head to foot. Here is the promise he gave:

But you will receive power when the Holy Spirit comes on you; and you will be my witnesses in Jerusalem, and in all Judea and Samaria, and to the ends of the earth.

Acts 1:8

▶ Whether you have read Acts 2:1–13 many times or it is new to you it is a very significant passage that is often misunderstood or confuses people. So take a moment to share together in your own personal language who the Holy Spirit is to you.

PRAYER
Lord we thank you for the promise of your presence with us as we learn and read your word together. We know that your Holy Spirit is an essential part of our lives. We have been open with each other about our questions and our doubts. Yet we sit with open hands of faith to receive your word and grow in that faith as we learn to understand and trust your promises. Come, Holy Spirit, and speak to us. Amen

Our study seeks to help us understand what it means to live in the fulfilment of that promise of Acts 1:8. We are considering what we call the day of Pentecost and thinking about Luke's description of some extraordinary events. We shall consider:

▶ *The circumstances* – what actually took place?
▶ *The significance* – what does it mean?

1. The circumstances
Luke's account details three distinct elements.

A particular time (Acts 2:1)
Luke anchors the event at a particular point in time – this didn't happen on any day of the week but on the day of Pentecost. We automatically associate this with the Christian festival but Luke is sending a different signal. Long before it was a Christian festival it was a Jewish celebration.

In the Jewish calendar this was the middle celebration of three harvest festivals. It was sometimes called *the feast of weeks* as it was held seven weeks after the first harvest festival. Seven weeks is around 50 days, which is where the name pentecost originates – *pente* is Greek for 50.

There appears to be some significance about the timing of this event – and we shall think more about this later.

A powerful experience (Acts 2:2–4)

The picture is of a powerful, supernatural mystical experience and one which Luke appears to struggle to describe. His use of words such as 'a sound like ...' (2:2) and 'what seemed to be' (2:3) suggests he ran short of vocabulary to describe what took place. The group of disciples were together in a house in Jerusalem (perhaps the same place where Jesus shared a farewell meal with his friends?) when the sound of a gale force wind filled the building, tongues of flames of fire appeared and rested on the occupants who suddenly began to speak in other languages. This was not contrived or planned but a sudden and supernatural event where the initiative was taken by God himself.

> ▶ Ask people to try and put themselves in the situation and say how they think they would have reacted. This can be helpful because we can over read this passage and lose any sense of the impact of it or it is so freaky that we cannot connect with it at all. Encourage people to be honest making it clear that there really are no right answers!

A public response (Acts 2:5–13)

What started as a private affair ends up a public event. Luke skips the details of how this happened – we are simply told that a crowd gathered (2:6) in response to the noise. Jerusalem was full of Jews from across the Greek/Roman world who were attending the festival. They were astonished at what they saw and heard – people from Galilee were fluently talking about God in the native languages of the crowd. Luke gives a long list (2:9–11) of those who were present to witness such an extraordinary scene. We can imagine the response if a group of people from Italy, France, Russia, Brazil and Pakistan could suddenly hear a group of untrained people fluently speaking their language and declaring the greatness of God.

Many were shaken by what they witnessed and asked some deep questions. Others made a joke of it because cynicism is always the refuge of the insecure (2:12–13).

Perhaps an important point we can draw is that this was not some private praise party for a favoured few – ordinary people were caught up by what took place within the remarkable events of the day of Pentecost.

- Look at the passage and see how different groups of people were affected: the disciples in the house; the crowds of God-fearing Jews staying in Jerusalem; and the other onlookers.
- Describe an occasion when something out of the ordinary happened at your church. This may have been a funeral or community service with many visitors where there was a deep sense of God's presence. How did it affect the regular congregation; those who had a vague connection to the church and those who heard about it on the grapevine (the onlookers).

We begin to see God's Holy Spirit working in dramatic ways in a public arena and not just serving the private needs of the church congregation.

2. The significance
It may help if we consider the events of the day of Pentecost in two ways:

- What did it mean then?
- What does it mean now?

What did it mean then?
We need look no further than Peter's impromptu sermon to find the answer to this question (2:14–40). When he got out of bed that morning he would hardly have expected he would end up preaching in the open air about Jesus and then witnessing the baptism of 3,000 new believers! (2:41)

READ Acts 2:14–41
This is a long passage – but keep it flowing and imagine the scene.

> Then Peter stood up with the Eleven, raised his voice and addressed the crowd: "Fellow Jews and all of you who live in Jerusalem, let me explain this to you; listen carefully to what I say. These men are not drunk, as you suppose. It's only nine in the morning! No, this is what was spoken by the prophet Joel:
>
> "'In the last days, God says, I will pour out my Spirit on all people. Your sons and daughters will prophesy, your young men will see visions, your old men will dream dreams. Even on my servants, both men and women, I will pour out my Spirit in those days, and they will prophesy. I will show wonders in the heaven above and signs on the earth below, blood and fire and billows of smoke. The sun will be turned to darkness and the moon to blood before the coming of the great and glorious day of the Lord. And everyone who calls on the name of the Lord will be saved.'

"Men of Israel, listen to this: Jesus of Nazareth was a man accredited by God to you by miracles, wonders and signs, which God did among you through him, as you yourselves know. This man was handed over to you by God's set purpose and foreknowledge; and you, with the help of wicked men, put him to death by nailing him to the cross. But God raised him from the dead, freeing him from the agony of death, because it was impossible for death to keep its hold on him. David said about him:

"'I saw the Lord always before me. Because he is at my right hand, I will not be shaken. Therefore my heart is glad and my tongue rejoices; my body also will live in hope, because you will not abandon me to the grave, nor will you let your Holy One see decay. You have made known to me the paths of life; you will fill me with joy in your presence.'

"Brothers, I can tell you confidently that the patriarch David died and was buried, and his tomb is here to this day. But he was a prophet and knew that God had promised him on oath that he would place one of his descendants on his throne. Seeing what was ahead, he spoke of the resurrection of the Christ, that he was not abandoned to the grave, nor did his body see decay. God has raised this Jesus to life, and we are all witnesses of the fact. Exalted to the right hand of God, he has received from the Father the promised Holy Spirit and has poured out what you now see and hear. For David did not ascend to heaven, and yet he said,

"'The Lord said to my Lord: Sit at my right hand until I make your enemies a footstool for your feet.'

"Therefore let all Israel be assured of this: God has made this Jesus, whom you crucified, both Lord and Christ."

When the people heard this, they were cut to the heart and said to Peter and the other apostles, "Brothers, what shall we do?"

Peter replied, "Repent and be baptised, every one of you, in the name of Jesus Christ for the forgiveness of your sins. And you will receive the gift of the Holy Spirit. The promise is for you and your children and for all who are far off—for all whom the Lord our God will call."

With many other words he warned them; and he pleaded with them, "Save yourselves from this corrupt generation." Those who accepted his message were baptised, and about three thousand were added to their number that day.

Peter's sermon bears careful reading. Luke only offers a few notes on what was obviously a powerful message. Peter began with an explanation as to the significance of what had just taken place. Referring to a quotation from the Old Testament prophet Joel (Acts 2:16–21 and Joel 2:28–32), Peter declared – Jesus has kept his promise. 'This is that' was his theme. God promised that in the last days his Holy Spirit would be poured out on all people and this is the fulfilment of that promise. Peter skilfully links all this to the person of Jesus, his death and resurrection pointing his listeners to believe in him and receive the twin gifts of forgiveness and the Holy Spirit (2:38).

As we look back at the final instructions Jesus gave his followers it is clear that they were to wait in Jerusalem until the Holy Spirit came on them in power and then their mission to the world would commence (Acts 1:4–9). Peter addressed the crowd in the belief that Jesus had kept his promise.

> ▶ Look at Acts 1:8. Imagine being Peter and the disciples and being witnesses on the day of Pentecost. How would they now see Jesus?
> ▶ By God keeping his promises in such a way how does that help us to see the significance of Jesus?
> ▶ How does that impact our lives and our church's mission in respect to the promises of Jesus?

What does it mean now?
The day of Pentecost was a once-for-all event that marked the coming of God's Spirit in power. But it has an abiding significance for the followers of Christ in every generation. It is not simply a fascinating piece of history.

Two important truths flow from this passage:

▶ the baptism with the Holy Spirit and
▶ the beginning of world mission

The baptism with the Holy Spirit
Jesus himself described what would happen to his followers in these words: 'in a few days you will be baptised with the Holy Spirit' (1:5). Jesus compares this to John the Baptist plunging people into water as a sign of their desire to turn from their sins and follow God. The word to *baptise* means to *cover* or *submerge* and Jesus uses this as a picture of his followers being covered by the Holy Spirit.

The disciples had already received the Holy Spirit when Jesus breathed on them during one of his resurrection appearances (John 20:22). Some have suggested this was a prophetic enactment as Jesus breathed on the disciples and said in effect, 'You will receive the Holy Spirit at some stage in the future'. But the way the sentence is phrased in Greek makes that impossible. Jesus was giving a command and said, 'Receive now, the Holy Spirit'.

What occurred on the day of Pentecost was that the Holy Spirit came and clothed the disciples with power to be witnesses for Christ – just as Jesus had promised (Acts 1:8).

Some have argued that this means that a Christian needs a 'second blessing' experience of the Holy Spirit. Conversion to Christ is the first blessing and being baptised with the Holy Spirit is the second. But that two-stage approach does not always follow – take the story of the Roman officer Cornelius as an example (Acts 11:15–17). For some of us a radical experience of the Holy Spirit occurred after we had been Christians some time – but not all of us have the same story. The important lesson that we draw is that we all need the empowering of the Holy Spirit to enable us to live witnessing lives. Some of those caught up in the events of the day of Pentecost were filled again with the Holy Spirit (Acts 4:31) and Paul writes that all Christians should continually 'be filled with the Holy Spirit' (Eph. 5:18).

The evangelist D.L. Moody was once criticised for always praying, 'Lord, fill me again with your Spirit'. He was asked why he kept asking for something God had already given him. Moody replied, 'I keep asking because I leak a lot!'

We are reminded of our continual need for the power of God's Holy Spirit at work in our lives.

The beginning of world mission
Various arguments have been put forward concerning the significance of the timing of the coming of the Holy Spirit in power on the day of Pentecost. Some have seen it as the reversal of the Tower of Babel when earthly languages were confused (Gen. 11), others point to Pentecost being a time when Jews commemorated Moses receiving the law (or Torah) but now someone greater than Moses has come with a message of truth and grace – Jesus (John 1:17). There may well be several connecting points with the relevance of the day of Pentecost but it seems a central idea is that of harvest.

The Jews marked their agricultural year with three harvest festivals: *the Feast of Unleavened Bread* which marked the start of the barley harvest; *Pentecost* – or the Feast of Weeks – which marked the wheat harvest; and *the Feast of Ingathering* – which marked the end of the agricultural year.

The first of these was close to Passover – the time when Jesus was crucified and the last has echoes of Jesus teaching about the harvest of the end of the age (Matt. 13:24–30; 36–43). The suggestion is that the beginning of the harvest of God's new society of called-out people was marked by the death and resurrection of Jesus – and the end of the age will mark the final harvest. So Pentecost signifies the start of the harvest for those Christ has called to bear faithful witness to him. One description given to the Holy Spirit – the third person of the trinity – is *God the evangelist*. The significance of Pentecost then is seen in the mission call of the church to make known the love of Christ to the world.

The significance of the gift of the Holy Spirit is not primarily about personal blessing but it is about service for Christ in the world.

The promise of power was for action.

> ▶ Where do you/your church actively need the Holy Spirit's power at the moment?
> ▶ What world situations can you see that have a desperate need for the Holy Spirit's power to be active?

SUMMING UP
Our study brings both a word of encouragement and challenge as we consider the gift of God's Holy Spirit.

The **encouragement** is that we are not alone. Jesus has sent his Spirit to lead, guide, teach, strengthen and help us. He is the *Paraclete* – the helper, counsellor and comforter (see what Jesus said about him in John 14:15–27). Sometimes in an airport or shopping centre we come across an escalator or mechanical walkway that takes the strain out of covering a long distance. In the same way the Holy Spirit carries us forward to achieve all that God has for us.

The **challenge** is that we need to resist the temptation to rely on our own resources. Western Christians in particular have a tendency to think that money, manpower and human ingenuity are all that is needed to undertake the task of making Jesus known. The first followers of Christ were badly under-resourced and yet turned their world upside down. We need the power of God's Holy Spirit if we are to fulfil all he has for us to do. Without him, we can do nothing of lasting worth.

The state of Texas is famous for its oil industry and one of its legendary oil wells is named *Yates Pool*. The land was owned for some years by the Yates family who – in the dark days of the Depression – lived in abject poverty. Through the kindness of friends and family these farmers made it through – but only just. Years later as oil companies were looking to buy land they asked the family if they could drill some est wells on the property. At 1,115 feet they struck oil and that single well produced 30,000 barrels of oil per day for over 30 years.

The family had lived as paupers when beneath their feet there lay resources beyond their wildest imaginings.

The challenge of our study is this: how do we face the task of serving Christ in our world? With our own meagre resources or with his unlimited supply? Far better to live as people of promise than as people who rely on themselves.

DURING THE WEEK

Commit to pray for one another as you live out the promise of power in the coming weeks.

Commit to pray for those world situations that you have identified as needing the power of God to intervene and report back on what happens in the next seven days.

PRAYER

Take time to pray that you will be filled with the Holy Spirit. You may like to use the words of Moody and say together:

Lord giver of all good gifts
Thank you for the wonderful gift of the Holy Spirit
Together we ask you, "Fill us with your Holy Spirit".
Amen

PEOPLE OF HOPE

AIM: To hold fast to our hope in time of change

READ Acts 20:17-38

From Miletus, Paul sent to Ephesus for the elders of the church. When they arrived, he said to them: "You know how I lived the whole time I was with you, from the first day I came into the province of Asia. I served the Lord with great humility and with tears, although I was severely tested by the plots of the Jews. You know that I have not hesitated to preach anything that would be helpful to you but have taught you publicly and from house to house. I have declared to both Jews and Greeks that they must turn to God in repentance and have faith in our Lord Jesus.

"And now, compelled by the Spirit, I am going to Jerusalem, not knowing what will happen to me there. I only know that in every city the Holy Spirit warns me that prison and hardships are facing me. However, I consider my life worth nothing to me, if only I may finish the race and complete the task the Lord Jesus has given me— the task of testifying to the gospel of God's grace.

"Now I know that none of you among whom I have gone about preaching the kingdom will ever see me again. Therefore, I declare to you today that I am innocent of the blood of all men. For I have not hesitated to proclaim to you the whole will of God. Keep watch over yourselves and all the flock of which the Holy Spirit has made you overseers. Be shepherds of the church of God, which he bought with his own blood. I know that after I leave, savage wolves will come in among you and will not spare the flock. Even from your own number men will arise and distort the truth in order to draw away disciples after them. So be on your guard! Remember that for three years I never stopped warning each of you night and day with tears.

"Now I commit you to God and to the word of his grace, which can build you up and give you an inheritance among all those who are sanctified. I have not coveted anyone's silver or gold or clothing. You yourselves know that these hands of mine have supplied my own needs and the needs of my companions.

In everything I did, I showed you that by this kind of hard work we must help the weak, remembering the words the Lord Jesus himself said: 'It is more blessed to give than to receive.'

When he had said this, he knelt down with all of them and prayed. They all wept as they embraced him and kissed him. What grieved them most was his statement that they would never see his face again. Then they accompanied him to the ship.

SET THE SCENE

Our final study from Acts takes us to the farewell speech Paul makes to a group of church leaders. It is unusual for several reasons. It is the only address in the book of Acts that is given to an audience made up exclusively of Christians. Luke who wrote this account was present when the address was given and what we are reading is an eyewitness (or earwitness!) record. It was given to the leaders of the church at Ephesus – but not in their home city. They had travelled for several days to meet Paul at his request at a place called Miletus. It is a farewell speech as Paul knew that he would not meet these friends again on earth.

Paul was travelling en route to Jerusalem and had in mind a particular deadline (20:16) but felt a keen sense of responsibility to the church he had invested in at Ephesus. His travel route could have taken him through this famous seaport but Paul knew he would be held up by seeing people so he made the conscious decision to go straight to the port of Miletus which was south of Ephesus and ask the leaders of the church to travel to meet him there. Such a journey will have taken them several days but they sensed, no doubt, that such a summons from someone who had been so influential in their early history had to be important.

Lord Randolph Churchill once described the distinguished politician Gladstone as 'an old man in a hurry'. The inference was for people to watch out as Gladstone was acting like a man on borrowed time. That description would seem to sum up Paul's mood as he prepares to speak to some very dear friends.

We may expect such a sad parting to be painful (and it was not without tears) yet the message we are studying reminds why we are called to live as people of hope. Our study will consider the three main themes of Paul's farewell message:

- Paul and the past
- Paul and the future
- Paul and his goodbye

> ▶ Paul was preparing to leave people and a place that he was very attached to. Describe some of the partings that you have had to do. Talk about your past in that place and the people you left. How did you see the future and the changes that lay ahead of you? How do you cope with goodbyes?

1. Paul and the past (Acts 20:17–21)

Paul had spent around three years in Ephesus and had seen many of the church come to faith in Christ. Some of the elders who now sat with Paul may well have been appointed by him and had received their grounding in the faith through his teaching and influence.

Paul reminds them of some of the hallmarks of his ministry in Ephesus.

Humility (20:19) he had come to them as a servant with a willingness to do anything that would bring them spiritual benefit.

Tears (20:19) it had not been an easy task and Paul had known dark and lonely times.

Opposition (20:19) some of the leaders of the Jewish community had it in for Paul and had consistently plotted against him.

Diligence (20:20) Paul had worked hard during his time in Ephesus visiting homes and teaching publicly making sure that his friends had a firm grasp of their faith.

Christ-centredness (20:21) Paul reminds his friends of the heart of his message – he told everyone he met whatever their background that they needed to change direction and follow Jesus.

On a first reading Paul's summary of his time in Ephesus may seem over the top and quite defensive. To understand Paul's motives we need to remember two things. First, there were those who opposed him and steadfastly criticised his ministry often accusing him of self-interest. He may have had these people in mind when he spoke about troublemakers coming into the church (20:29). Second, he is passing on the torch of responsible leadership to these elders and is giving them a solemn reminder of the example he has set and expects them to follow.

▶ All of us lead in some way and influence others whether in our work or family or church. You may be a grandparent, office manager, church leader, council member, mum/dad, carer. Spend a moment thinking about your leadership responsibilities with these hallmarks in mind.

Humility – do others see you as humble? Do you perceive yourself as humble?

Tears – recognise the difficult times and the frustrations that leading can bring.

Opposition – if you have clear opposition then recognise it and quietly spend a moment praying for those who oppose you and for yourself as you deal with them.

Diligence – assess how diligent you are in your leading role.

Christ-centredness – Paul reminds his friends to tell everyone they meet that they need to change direction and follow Jesus.

▶ Think of new ways you can lead in a Christ-centred way in the week ahead by making one significant action.

2. Paul and the future (Acts 20:22–27)

Paul turns to the topic of the future – both his own and that of the church at Ephesus.

Paul's future

Compulsion (20:22–23) Paul is travelling to Jerusalem with a strong sense of conviction that the Lord is directing his steps.

Completion (20:24) He knows that he faces great hardships but is committed to fulfil the work Jesus gave him.

Conclusion (20:25–27) Paul will not see his friends again on earth but tells them that he has faithfully discharged all that Christ had called him to do. (To understand what he means by claiming to be 'innocent of the blood of all men' read Ezekiel 33:1–9.)

Their future

Shepherds (20:28) Paul reminds these leaders that the Holy Spirit has called them to their important task and that they need to undertake it with great integrity watching their own lives as well as the congregation.

Sheep (20:28) They have been called ('the Holy Spirit has made you overseers') to lead people who are valuable to Christ ('bought with his own blood') and belong to the family of God ('the church of God'). Leadership must be treated as a solemn trust and handled with great care.

Wolves (20:29–31) Paul gives a solemn warning about those who will try and wreck the valuable work that has taken place in Ephesus. Experience shows that Satan's tactics seldom vary. Most attacks centre on false teaching, people building their own empire or those who are simply troublemakers. Paul reminds them to stay alert and remember his example.

GET REAL ABOUT LIFE IN THE LOCAL CHURCH

The analogy of shepherds and sheep can, if we are not careful, lead to an over-romantic and totally unrealistic view of local church life. John Stott rescues us from that with this timely reminder:

Sheep are not all the clean, cuddly creatures they may appear. In fact they are dirty, subject to unpleasant pests and regularly need to be dipped in strong chemicals to rid them of lice, ticks and worms. They are also unintelligent, wayward and obstinate.

The Message of Acts, John Stott (IVP, 1994, p 329)

▶ Think about your church and how you can support the shepherds recognising the challenge of their task.
▶ John Stott's description of sheep is very helpful. Read the description and talk about what resonates with your church community at the moment. You may feel you recognise yourself in that description – maybe you can be bold enough to say so.
▶ Importantly – move on and talk about what ways such insights can help as you consider the future of your church and its realistic vision and goals?

3. Paul and his goodbye (Acts 20:32–38)

This must have been a heart-rending moment charged with emotion (20:37) as Paul said his final words of farewell. Not many find 'goodbyes' easy but Paul's emphatic assertion that they would never see him on earth again must have hit very hard (20:38).

Yet the 'goodbye' was charged with positive encouragement.

Hope (20:32) Paul is able to commit his friends to the gracious hands of God; understanding and living this message of grace can make them strong and hold them fast no matter what problems may lay ahead. Paul did not see the church at Ephesus (or anywhere else for that matter) as his property. Paul's understanding of how churches grow (1 Cor. 3:5–9) gave him confidence that the good work could continue after he was gone.

- Imagine that you have just heard that your well-loved leader is leaving. Identify the good work that the Lord has done through him or her and think of ways you can carry it on. It is important at times of loss and goodbyes to remember and recognise the hope that comes from all that God has done, is doing and will do.

Hard work (20:33–35) Paul reminds them of his own example during the time he lived at Ephesus. No one could accuse him of using his position for financial gain. Far from it, he worked hard to supply his own needs alongside tackling all his responsibilities as a missionary and church planter. Such a challenge would counteract any attitude among these leaders that would suggest they could sit back and take things easy. Leading a local church (if it is done well) is always hard work.

- Pray for all the leaders in your church/other churches in your area and those who take a national or world lead. They need your prayers. It is hard work.

Helpfulness (20:35) Paul links his hard work on behalf of weaker people with a forgotten saying of Jesus. He quotes a statement from the Lord that appears nowhere in any of the four gospels. Paul may have been quoting from a document containing sayings of Jesus or he could have heard it first hand from one of the disciples who heard these memorable words: 'It is more blessed to give than to receive' (20:35). Paul could not have concluded his farewell on a better note. All who follow Christ are called to walk as Jesus walked (1 John 2:6).

SUMMING UP

We can often be discouraged by events and circumstances. Sometimes life in a local congregation can be tough. Paul's farewell address to the Ephesian church leaders serves as a reminder that even in sad and difficult times we can find God's grace. Five lessons in particular stand out.

The value of strong relationships

The reason there were tears in this emotional scene of saying 'goodbye' is that these people really cared about each other. Paul was more than a pastor who spent some years with them early in their history for they considered him a brother and a member of their family. Strong churches are built on authentic relationships that go beyond committee structures and appointments. We need to invest in building these kind of relationships.

- What sort of friendships are encouraged in your church and how are they best built?

God's work is bigger than one individual

Changes in local church leadership often produce insecurity. How will we cope? How can that person ever be replaced? Will life ever be the same again? We notice how Paul's task as a leader is to encourage independence from him rather than dependence on him. Skilled leaders work to the Ephesians 4 model of leadership where God's people are equipped to serve and not simply to be served (Eph. 4:11–13).

> ▶ Is there a sense of the people in your church being equipped to serve? Can you see that happening and how can it happen more?

The importance of walking in God's will

If Paul's motivation was to keep everyone happy then he would not have insisted on travelling to Jerusalem. He could have saved his friends tears not only in Ephesus but in Tyre (Acts 21:3–6) and Caesarea (Acts 21:8–14). Paul was set on obedience to the Lord Jesus as the primary goal of his life. This is a challenging reminder that discipleship is not about doing our own thing or pleasing others – but obeying Christ.

> ▶ The Christian life is not about trying to keep everyone happy, but bringing God's love and redemption to all those around you. Sometimes that can be painful and challenging. Note one way that God is challenging you to a deeper discipleship. Note one way that God is challenging your church to a deeper discipleship.

The need to be on our guard

Paul's warning about wolves attacking the flock is a timely reminder about vigilance. His assertion that false teaching and bad influence can arise within the congregation itself is another clear signal. Wrong thinking, divisive attitudes and personal power struggles didn't die out with the 1st century church. Such a lesson needn't make us paranoid but it should cause us to be prayerful – and very alert.

> ▶ Commit each member of the group to pray for your church on a particular day of the coming week – for protection, unity, and to be sustained by and able to bring strong Christian hope.

The power of God's grace

Paul believed that the message of God's grace in Christ was sufficient to keep his friends faithful and moving forward, Perhaps that is why his letter to the whole church at Ephesus (plus other congregations in the region) has grace as its theme. The first part of the letter (Eph. 1–3) is about the message of grace explained and the remainder (Eph. 4–6) deals with grace applied. He knows that understanding and applying the good news of the Lord Jesus Christ can build people up in their faith and make strong disciples.

As the leaders of the church at Ephesus made their journey home their hearts must have been heavy. But according to some early church traditions John, one of Jesus' closest disciples, made his home in Ephesus. Irenaeus, a leader of a later generation wrote: 'John the disciple of the Lord .... published the gospel while he was residing at Ephesus in Asia.' (Quoted in Arthur G. Patzia, *The Emergence of the Church: Context, Growth, Leadership & Worship*, IVP, 2001, p. 130)

If this was the case then the church received the rich benefit of one who had lived so close to Christ being part of their family. There is a tradition that holds that Mary the mother of our Lord stayed in Ephesus under John's care. If that is true it would have proved a double blessing to the church.

All of which serves as a reminder that even in the most difficult times we can trust the Lord Jesus to work out his plan and purpose for his people. He knows what he is doing even when we can't fully understand all that is happening. His love for us is unquenchable come what may (Rom. 8:28–39).

That is why Christians above all others must live as people of hope.

PRAYER
At the conclusion of this study reflect on the time that you have spent studying Acts Talk together about how you would finish off the following sentences. You may like to give each sentence to a pair of people and ask them to chat over their responses together. At the end of the session draw the group together and pray that God will enable you to put into practice what you have talked about.

As people of vision our vision for our church is to ...
As people of passion our passion as a church is to be ...
As people of courage our church will be seen as ...
As people of faith our church will grow as we ...
As people of commitment our church will be committed to ...
As people of promise we undertake to ...
As people of hope we will continue to ...

Conclude by saying the grace together.

> *The grace of our Lord Jesus Christ*
> *And the love of God and the fellowship of the Holy Spirit*
> *Be with us all, ever more.*   Amen

LEADERS' GUIDE

TO HELP YOU LEAD

You may have led a group many times before or this may be your first time. Here is some advice on how to lead these studies:

▶ As a group leader, you don't have to be an expert or a lecturer. You are there to facilitate the learning of the group members – helping them to discover for themselves the wisdom in God's word.

▶ You do need to be aware of the group's dynamics, however. People can be quite quick to label themselves and each other in a group situation. One person might be seen as the expert, another the moaner who always has something to complain about. Be aware of the different types of individuals in the group. You may need to encourage those who find it hard to get a word in, and quieten down those who always have something to say. Talk to members between sessions to find out how they feel about the group.

▶ Adapt the questions for your group as you feel is appropriate. Some groups may know each other very well and will be prepared to talk at a deep level. New groups may take a bit of time to get to know each other before making themselves vulnerable. You probably won't be able to tackle all the questions in each session so decide in advance which ones are most appropriate to your group and situation.

▶ Encourage everyone to ask questions, voice doubts and discuss difficulties. Your group should be a safe place to be honest. If discussion doesn't resolve the issue, ask everyone to pray about it between sessions, and ask your minister for advice.

▶ Delegate as much as you like! The easiest activities to delegate are reading the text, and the prayer sessions, but there are other ways to involve the group members. Giving people responsibility can help them own the session much more.

▶ Pray for group members by name, that God would meet with them during the week. Pray for the group session that it will be a constructive and helpful time. Ask the Lord to equip you as you lead the group.

THE STRUCTURE OF EACH SESSION

Feedback: find out what people remember from the previous session and if they have been able to act during the week on what was discussed last time.

To set the scene: an activity or a question to get everyone thinking about the subject to be studied.

Bible reading: it's important to actually read the passage you are studying during the session. Ask someone to prepare this in advance or go around the group reading a verse or two each. But don't assume everyone will be happy to read out loud.

Questions: these are designed to promote discussion on how to apply what the passage says to your individual/group situation.

During the week: a specific task to do during the week to help people put into practice what they have learned.

Prayer: suggestions for creative prayer. Use these suggestions alongside other group expressions of worship such as singing. Add a prayer time with opportunities to pray for group members and their families and friends.

GROUND RULES

How do people know what is expected of them during your meetings? Is it ever discussed, or do they just pick up clues from each other? You may find it helpful to discuss some ground rules for the house group at the start of this course, even if your group has been going a long time. This also gives you an opportunity to talk about how you, as the leader, see the group. Ask everyone to think about what they want to get out of the course. How do they want the group to work? What values do they want to be part of the group's experience: honesty, respect, confidentiality? How do they want their contributions to be treated? You could ask everyone to write down three ground rules on slips of paper and put them in a bowl. Pass the bowl around the group. Each person takes out a rule and reads it, and someone collates the list. Discuss the ground rules that have been suggested and come up with a top five. This method enables everyone to contribute fairly anonymously. Alternatively, if your group are all quite vocal, have a straight discussion about it!